Excavations In Eastern Crete: Vrokastro

Edith Hall Dohan

UNIVERSITY OF PENNSYLVANIA
THE MUSEUM
ANTHROPOLOGICAL PUBLICATIONS
VOL. III   NO. 3

EXCAVATIONS IN EASTERN CRETE
VROKASTRO

BY

E. H. HALL

PHILADELPHIA
PUBLISHED BY THE UNIVERSITY MUSEUM
1914

UNIVERSITY OF PENNSYLVANIA

THE MUSEUM

ANTHROPOLOGICAL PUBLICATIONS

VOL. III   No. 3

EXCAVATIONS IN EASTERN CRETE
VROKASTRO

BY

E. H. HALL

PHILADELPHIA
PUBLISHED BY THE UNIVERSITY MUSEUM
1914

CONTENTS.

EXCAVATIONS IN EASTERN CRETE, VROKASTRO.

INTRODUCTION.

During the last decade and a half, the excavations which have been carried on in the island of Crete have been confined almost entirely to sites dating from the bronze age. The splendid results of these excavations are now so well known as to need no recapitulation. Successive stages have been traced in the history of a brilliant civilization which had its rise in a remote era of the third millennium and maintained itself until the closing centuries of the second millennium B. C. It is only natural that while the attention of the archæological world has been focused on these Minoan discoveries the more primitive culture of the succeeding age of iron should have received less than its due share of honor. Pottery ornamented with geometric patterns, the characteristic product of the iron age, has been found in abundance in Cretan soil, but of the vases decorated in this geometric style which have been brought into the Candia Museum, many, found by peasants, have not been published at all; others, unearthed by archæologists, have been but scantily described and inadequately reproduced.[1]

---

[1] The principal publications dealing with geometric remains of Crete are: Orsi, *A. J. A.*, 1897, pp. 251–265; Boyd, *A. J. A.*, 1901, pp. 125–157; Halbherr and Mariani, *id.*, pp. 259–314; Hogarth, *B. S. A.* VI, pp. 82–85; Bosanquet, *id.* VIII, pp. 231–251; Droop, *id.* XII, pp. 24–62; Mackenzie, *id.* XIII, pp. 428–445; Mariani, *Mon. Ant.* VI, pp. 342–348 and Pl. XII, 58–62; Halbherr, *id.* XII, pp. 114–118; Wide, *Jahrbuch*, 1899, pp. 35–43; *Athen. Mitt.* XXII, pp. 233–258.

There have not been wanting, however, scholars who have realized the importance of this period; Dr. Duncan Mackenzie in his masterly analysis of the pottery of the early iron age[1] has indicated the probable place of the Achæan invasion in the series of inroads by northerners into the island.   Certainly it is by a detailed study of the remains of this epoch that the relations of the Minoan culture to that of classical Greece may best be determined.   The more exact our knowledge of this period, the clearer our conception of the extent and date of invasions intermediate between the fall of Minoan power and the dawn of classical Greece.

It was in the hope of throwing light on such problems of ethnology and chronology that excavations were undertaken for the University Museum at a lofty site called Vrokastro.   This hill had been visited by Mrs. C. H. Hawes and Mr. R. B. Seager in 1903 and, on the evidence of numerous walls and of sherds picked up on the surface, had been regarded as a promising place for geometric remains.   Two campaigns were devoted to this site; the earlier in 1910 lasted but three weeks, the second was carried on during May and June, 1912.   The number of men employed ranged from twenty-five to sixty, according to whether houses or tombs were being dug, a smaller number being required for tombs.   The men who worked with picks and knives were mostly veterans trained at previous excavations; the rest of the force was enrolled at the neighboring village of Kalo Khorio (Καλὸ Χωριό).   The work was under the supervision of the writer; she was, however, greatly aided by the advice of Mr. Seager, who paid frequent visits to the excavations. To Mr. Seager's courtesy the expedition was also indebted for the loan of excavation tents, for the use of his house at Pacheia

[1] *Loc. cit.*

Ammos as headquarters, and for help in the difficult matter of procuring supplies.   It is a pleasure also to acknowledge the kindness of Mr. Hagidakis and Mr. Xanthoudides, who, as heretofore, did all in their power to aid the Museum's work in Crete.

Vrokastro[1] (Βρόκαστρο), a shortened form of Ἑβραιό-καστρο, is the name given to a steep limestone spur which rises to a height of nearly a thousand feet on the east side of the green and picturesque valley of Kalo Khorio.   Its north and west faces are scarcely accessible, but on the east there is a winding path used by goatherds and by those who cultivate the small terraces built here and there against the mountain-side.   The south face is connected by a saddle with the hills behind.   With the exception of a few of the steepest crags, this entire mountain, from the summit to the sea, is strewn with potsherds.   House-walls and retaining walls may also be traced among the bushes, and enough of these have been examined to show that they belong to the geometric period.   The appearance of Vrokastro at the height of its power must have been similar to that of an Italian hilltown of to-day.

That so steep and barren a mountain should have been chosen as a place of human abode invites speculation.   Two reasons present themselves.   To a people living in fear of sudden invasion by sea, Vrokastro presented marked advantages.   The north face of the mountain is broken by crags and pointed pinnacles of rock which would have served admirably as lookouts.

---

[1] This is a common place-name in Greek lands, cf. Pernot, *Melodies populaires grecques de l'isle de Chio*, song 48, p. 63:

ὅλα τὰ κάστρα ἐπῆγα, κάστρ' ἐγύρισα
σὰν τῆς Ἑβριᾶς τὸ κάστρο, κάστρο δὲν εἶδα.

Watchmen stationed here could have discerned boats far out at sea and could have signaled their approach to men sowing or harvesting in the plains below in time to allow them to reach safely the high retreat on the summit before the hostile boats were beached.   Moreover, Vrokastro was but a part of the iron age settlement.   On the hills to the south, especially on Karakovilia (Καρακοβίλια), which lies immediately behind and which is joined to Vrokastro by a saddle, were found both houses and tombs.   A circuit of five kilometers indeed would scarcely include the district where traces of geometric remains abound. For this entire area as well as for the valley of Kalo Khorio, Vrokastro would have served as a lookout and citadel.   Again, we may suppose that at some stage at least in the history of the site the valley had been seized by invaders who had reduced their predecessors to the position of *perioikoi* and driven them to the less promising districts like Vrokastro and the hills behind it.

The sketch map of Pl. XVII shows the relation of Vrokastro to the neighboring localities where excavations were carried on. With the exception of Kalo Khorio there is no village at any of these places; the names are given by Cretan custom to the land itself, each ridge, valley, or mountain-peak having its own special name.   Karakovilia, Mazi Khortia (Μαζυχορτιά), and Amigthali ('Αμυγδάλι) are three rough, upland moors as wild and rocky as Vrokastro but with less precipitous faces. Kopranes (Κοπράνες) is a foot-hill of Vrokastro and is only a little higher than the Kalo Khorio valley.

The short campaign of 1910 was devoted to the summit of Vrokastro in the hope that some trace of a shrine might there be brought to light.   Nothing, however, save the tangle

of house-walls shown in Pl. XVIII appeared.   The depth of
deposit, which was sometimes as much as three meters, seemed
remarkable for so bare and rugged a mountain.   The object
of the season's work in 1912 was first to clear more houses and
ascertain the date of the walls along the northern face of the
mountain, and secondly to find the tombs belonging to this
settlement.   The men were accordingly set to work at the
opening of the season to clear a stretch of hillside on the north
face of the mountain, some 100 meters below the summit.
The main force of workmen was occupied here for a month,
though now and again men were detailed either to sink trenches
adjacent to house-walls further down the slope or to try places
which promised well for tombs.

The very first day, in fact, a workman was sent to Karakovilia to a spot which had attracted my attention in 1910, but
which could not then be conveniently tested, inasmuch as it
lay beneath a guy rope of a tent.   The place was marked by
a pile of tumbled stones, and proved upon investigation to be
the site of a rectangular chamber-tomb.   It is somewhat doubtful whether the pile of stones which appeared on the surface
was really a part of the fallen roof of the tomb; it may have
been merely a chance occurrence.   The best clue, as we later
learned, for locating such tombs was the white, chalky soil
called "kouskoura," from which they were cut.   Most of them,
moreover, were built under the shelter of a ledge or projecting
spur of rock so that they might be protected against the
disasters of washouts.

It was hoped that with the discovery of this large chamber-
tomb, the cemetery of Vrokastro had been located and that the
finding of other tombs would be an easy task.   But such was
not the case.   Trial trenches sunk in the neighborhood of this

tomb revealed nothing but house-walls, and subsequent experience pointed also to the conclusion, that tombs had been interspersed among houses. Later in the season the workmen of the third class were sent away and the rest of the force began a systematic search for burials. As a result two more chamber-tombs and six bone-enclosures were found at Mazikhortia; another chamber-tomb, a cave burial, and a pithos interment were found at Amigthali; and both chamber-tombs and bone-enclosures were found further down the mountain at Kopranes. And everywhere, both adjacent to these tombs and in places where search for tombs was unsuccessful, house-walls of the geometric period constantly came to light. These were no more than tested except on Vrokastro in the spots already mentioned.

In several places Minoan remains were located, and first on Vrokastro itself, where the Minoan vases described below were found at a low level. North of the Kopranes graves, a Minoan house was dug which yielded Late Minoan I potsherds and a good sealstone. At Kato Arniko (Κάτω ᾿Αρνικό) an Early Minoan cave was cleared, and lastly, at a little promontory called Priniatiko Pirgo (Πρινιάτικο Πύργο), an extensive Minoan settlement was discovered which yielded during the week that excavations were carried on there, beautiful specimens of the Vasiliki mottled style, of rippled bowls, and of other Late Minoan I products, (Fig. 46). The pottery was splendidly preserved. The only disadvantage of this site as a place for future excavations is that the upper deposit dates from the Roman period, and that Roman walls have in many places cut into the Minoan remains. This promontory of Priniatiko Pirgo was doubtless the shipping station for a large Minoan town which must be sought further up the Kalo Khorio Valley near and under the present village of Kalo Khorio.   Excellent sherds of the Middle Minoan III and Late Minoan I periods were brought to us by peasants working the thick alluvial soil between the village and Kato Arniko.

Fig. 46.   Minoan Pottery from Priniatiko Pirgo (1 : 6).

Mention should also be made of an extensive Græco-Roman site located on the peninsula called Nisi (Νῆσι).   Coins of Aluntium are frequently found in this vicinity and it may be that this settlement should be so identified.

THE HOUSES.

ARCHITECTURE.

The houses uncovered on Vrokastro show a minimum of architectural skill. In both groups, that excavated in 1910 and that in 1912, there were few rooms which were either sufficiently regular in shape or large enough to constitute a dwelling-room that by modern civilized standards would be considered endurable. The reason is not far to seek. To erect symmetrical and spacious houses on Vrokastro would have involved an elaborate series of terraces that would have imposed a vast expenditure of time and labor on the most skilled builders. And the people of the iron age were not under favorable circumstances skilled builders. Some of the houses unearthed by Mrs. Hawes at Kavousi are, it is true, solidly and regularly constructed and the building found near the bone-enclosures on Karakovilia seems also to imply better methods, but in general it may be said that this people to an even greater extent than their predecessors of the bronze age were content to live in small and poorly constructed rooms.

Of the group of houses excavated in 1912, no plan was attempted. An amateur plan of that uncovered in 1910 is shown in Pl. XVIII. No elevation of the site was drawn, but the photograph of Pl. XXII shows the chief variations in level. The letters on the photograph refer to those on the plan.

The walls of Vrokastro are built of small stones with no other binding material than clay or mud daub. No bricks or squared stones appeared. Dressed stones, however, were found in the building on Karakovilia.   In several rooms upright faces of native rock served as a wall.   In such cases they were faced with rubble masonry which was remarkably well preserved.   This method of building can be paralleled in modern Cretan villages; in Kritsa the face of the steep rock against which the houses are built makes the fourth wall in more than one room.

Only one road about which there can be no dispute was found.   It is marked 2 on the plan, and probably led to the saddle connecting with the hills to the south.   Beside it was a drain built of small stones like those beside roads in Pseira. It is possible that 24 and 26 were also originally roads and that the walls of small stones built across them are of later origin.

There being thus no roads to divide the houses into blocks, it becomes quite impossible to distinguish separate houses.   In all probability the houses were built, like those on Pseira, in successive terraces, the part of the house on any one terrace not exceeding two stories in height.[1]   One well-preserved staircase is shown in Pl. XXIII, 3.

Some of the walls do not enclose rooms at all, but merely shut off the rocks where these emerge above the surface.   Rooms 17 and 19, *e. g.*, are both more regular in plan for the intervening rocks having been cut off by walls.   This method was, of course, easier than to remove the outcropping rock.   Where irregular surfaces of rock were lower than the floor to be built, a process of leveling up was employed.   The soil used to fill up such holes and crevices was of a reddish color, easily distinguishable from the brown soil of neighboring rooms.   It contained a large admixture of sherds of the type characteristic of the

---

[1] R. B. Seager, *University of Pennsylvania, The Museum, Anthropological Publications,* Vol. III, No. 1, *Excavations on the Island of Pseira, Crete,* p. 13.

very end of the bronze age, that to which the name Late Minoan III b has been given.[1]   The extremely uneven character of the rock as it appeared at the bottom of one room when entirely cleared, is shown in Pl. XXIII, 1.

The floors of the houses were made of trodden earth. Column bases occurred in three rooms.   In Room 34 a rec-

FIG. 47.   Sketch of Room 34, from Northeast, showing Rectangular Column
Basis above Rectangular Stone.

tangular column base was found, set upon another rectangular stone as foundation and for the purpose of raising the column base to the level of the native rock at the other end of the room, Fig. 47.   The sherds found at the level of this lower stone were of the Late Minoan III period.   The only object found above the floor was a large pithos of geometric date.

[1] Cf. Dawkins, *B. S. A.* X, p. 196.

STRATIFICATION.

The rubble walls of the Vrokastro houses were of little service in determining the periods in which the site was occupied. Occasionally it was possible to speak with certainty about the relative dates of juxtaposed walls, for a later wall was seen to be carried over an earlier. But usually there was no such criterion, nor were there any differences of construction observable, so that the determination of chronological periods was necessarily based on pottery. In connection with the subject of stratification, it will be convenient to describe the types of sherds yielded by the site.

The general rule for the stratification of Vrokastro was to find geometric or quasi-geometric sherds in the upper stratum, below these Late Minoan III sherds with occasionally Middle Minoan fragments at a still lower level. Neither remnants of pavements nor signs of trodden earth floors were detected to distinguish these various strata. The level of a floor could be inferred only from the unusual amount of pottery or from the presence of unbroken specimens. Not a single floor-level of the Late Minoan III period was so indicated. In the uppermost stratum the level of a geometric floor could frequently be fixed, and, in the lowest stratum, that of a Middle Minoan floor. In rooms like 26 and 27, where Middle Minoan vases were found nearly intact, it must be supposed that their owners had left them in the corners of the rooms, that they had become covered with dust and débris in the interval which elapsed before the occupation of the site in the Late Minoan III period and that they then became further buried in artificial fillings inserted to level up the uneven surface of these rooms. The greater part of the Mycenæan pottery came from such fillings.

These early deposits had sometimes been disturbed. In three cases Late Minoan III sherds were seen to overlie sherds of the geometric period. Such confusion was doubtless mainly due to the character of the site; in rooms built on sharply sloping ground material packed beneath floors, when once it came to be exposed to rains, would be carried down the hill and lodged against the lower wall of the room. This was precisely what happened in Room 17. In view, moreover, of the long period during which this site was occupied, it is natural to suppose that in antiquity some of these deposits beneath floors had been overturned in the process of rebuilding and of leveling up anew the very uneven surface of the hill.

Typical stratification was found in Room 27, where as usual the earth was stripped off a half meter at a time. In the first half meter was found geometric ware, principally bowls decorated with meanders, a few Late Minoan III sherds, the lamp of Fig. 57 d, and pieces of a small animal figure comparable to those in Fig. 56; in the second half meter, the Late Minoan III fragments were more numerous and with them began to appear Middle Minoan ware, notably fragments of cups and of larger vessels decorated with circular patches of dark paint connected with slanting lines; in the lowest half meter were a few Middle Minoan vases and a single sherd of Late Minoan III ware. Certain fillings were found to contain only Late Minoan III sherds; in Room 17, where a late wall had cut off a rectangular space, the earth within this space was found to contain nothing but Late Minoan III fragments, indicating that the later north wall of this room had been built at a time when sherds of this period were at hand for filling material. Similarly, in a room dug in 1912 which contained a pocket 2.50 deep, the red earth with which this hole had been filled contained Late Minoan III sherds with a single piece dating from the Middle Minoan I period.

The quantity of sherds yielded by the town-site was large, the harvest of a day's digging amounting oftentimes to thirty baskets. Over fifty per cent of these were unpainted, coming either from large pithoi or from smaller unpainted jars. The pithoi were decorated with a variety of stamped and moulded patterns shown in Fig. 48. Of the painted fabrics at least ninety per cent were of the geometric style. The rest were Minoan.

Sherds of typical Vrokastro fabrics are shown in Figs. 49-53.

Fig. 48.　Fragments of Pithoi with Stamped Ornaments from the Town (1 : 5)

Middle Minoan sherds are not here included, but illustrations of restored pieces of this period are shown in Figs. 64 and 66 and Pl. XXV, 1. The most common type of Middle Minoan I sherd is that already referred to, from a dark on light fabric decorated with circular patches of paint connected with slanting lines.[1] On Fig. 49 are shown typical sherds of a ware dating from the end of the bronze age. It will be seen at a glance that they are more Mycenæan than Minoan. Not once occurs the foliate pattern characteristic of the later stages of Knossian

---

[1] *University Museum, Anthropological Publications*, Vol. III, p. 19, Fig. 4, and p. 60, Fig. 32.

ceramic art.[1]   Instead are found the conventionalized buds, the stereotyped renderings of marine life, so familiar from the mainland.[2]   Many of these fragments, notably B, D, F, and I,

Fig. 49. Late Mycenæan Sherds from Town (1 : 2).

seem to be actual importations from the mainland; their good slip, finely polished surface, and lustrous paint suggest Furt-

[1] Evans, *Prehistoric Tombs of Knossos*, p. 120, Fig. 114, 55d.
[2] Cf. e.g. Furtwängler and Löschcke, *Mykenische Vasen*, Pl. IV, 27b XII; Pl. VI, 31 XII; and Pl. XXXIV, 342.

wängler and Löschcke's third style. Other pieces, like A with its muddled, senseless design, might equally well be a native product. Such pieces are analogous to the vases of the period of final abandonment at Palaikastro and the period of reoccupation at Gournia. Precisely the same type of pottery was found at Phylakopi, associated with the Mycenæan palace but coming from the very end of this palace period.[1]

The history of the main settlement on Vrokastro begins, therefore, in a period slightly posterior to that of the Zafer Papoura cemetery and contemporary with the end of the Mycenæan period at Phylakopi; or, in other words, in the period of the "widest diffusion" of Mycenæan art.

That this last phase of the art of the bronze age stands in the closest relation to that of the succeeding age of iron has been abundantly shown.[2] The excavations at Vrokastro evince fresh proof of this. From its output of sherds a series might be arranged which would show the gradual transition from the Late Minoan III or, more properly, the late Mycenæan style to the geometric style. In the matter of design the distinction is particularly hard to draw; the sherd on Fig. 50 H might be called either Mycenæan or geometric. In technique, however, the difference is more easily apparent and serves as the best means of distinguishing the two wares. The fine hard slip, the polished surface, and lustrous paint of the imported pieces and the native imitations of this technique are unknown in the geometric period, when a more porous clay was used which absorbed the thin paint of the design.

In Figs. 50–52 are shown typical sherds of the Vrokastrian geometric style. The stratification of the town site

---

[1] Phylakopi, Pl. XXXII, 1-10.
[2] Wide, Jahrbuch, 1899, pp. 35-43.

indicated no chronological distinction between the quasi-geometric style of Figs. 50 and 51 and the fully developed style

Fig. 50.   Sherds of the Quasi-Geometric Style from the Town (1 : 2).

of the sherds shown in Fig. 52.   Vases of both styles were found above floor levels.   Luckily the tombs supplanted here the evidence of the houses and showed that a line of demarcation

might be drawn between the two styles.   The patterns pecu-
liarly distinctive of the earlier quasi-geometric style are: triangles filled in solidly with black as in Fig. 50 E and Fig. 51 K;

Fig. 51. Sherds of the Quasi-Geometric Style from the Town (1 : 2).

upright ornaments filled in solidly with black and bounded
on one side by a straight line, on the other by a curved, Fig. 50 A
and Fig. 51 K, and edged frequently with a fringe of parallel

lines;[1] and circles in every form.   The circles are mathematically exact and are drawn with compasses; the larger circles are frequently embellished with triangles and checkers.   In this early stage of the geometric style, many curvilinear motives familiar in earlier decoration still persist.

Fig. 52.   Sherds of the Mature Geometric Style from the Town (4 : 9).

As the Mycenæan tradition weakened and foreign models were more frequently seen, the meander or partial meander became favorite motives, Figs. 51 E and 52 C, D, and E.

[1] This pattern occurs on a fragment from the Acropolis.   Graef, *Akropolis Vasen*, Taf. 9, 273.   Cf. also Schliemann, *Tiryns*, p. 133, No. 47.

This pattern is generally associated with a compact and mathematical arrangement of the ornament.   In this developed geometric style appear birds, human beings, and other motives characteristic of geometric vases elsewhere.

The last phase of Vrokastrian ceramic art is represented by a group of sherds in Fig. 53.   They were found in three different rooms but seem to come, with one exception, from a single vase.   The clay is pale green and covered with a buff slip; the interior is entirely covered with a fine lustrous black paint that recalls the fine black paint on the better class of Dipylon ware.   Fragments from the rim indicate that it was decorated with a row of squat birds, their wings represented by fringed lines.   The main field is divided into zones and filled with representations of chariots and warriors armed with helmets, shields, and swords.   According to the cursory method of the geometric style of drawing, the close-fitting cap of the helmet does not appear.[1]   The long conspicuous crest was evidently regarded as sufficient to indicate the entire helmet.   The shields are of the usual type, flaring at top and bottom and cut away in the center, a type which, according to Reichel, was superseded about the middle of the eighth century.[2]   The swords may be compared to those on a vase in Copenhagen.[3]   The chariots, as nearly as can be judged from these fragments, were drawn in a highly schematized manner, the floor of the chariot being entirely severed from the wheels.   These seem to have had four spokes.[4]   The stop-gap ornaments of these sherds are characteristic of the fully developed Dipylon style.

The sherd in Fig. 53 E is in technique quite similar to the

[1] Cf. Reichel, *Homerische Waffen*, pp. 109 and 110, Figs. 51 and 52.
[2] Reichel, *op. cit.*, p. 48, Fig. 25; *Jahrbuch*, 1899, p. 85, Fig. 44; and *Arch. Zeit.*, 1885, Pl. 8.
[3] *Arch. Zeit.*, 1885, Pl. 8.
[4] Cf. Reichel, *op. cit.*, pp. 124-125, Figs. 64-67.

fragments just described.   The panel to the right of the quatre-foil ornament was decorated with a bird.

The clay of these fragments was, as was stated, of a

Fig. 53.   Latest Type of Sherds from the Town.   All but E from One Vase (1 : 2).

greenish color.   That of the others in Figs. 50–52 shades in color from buff to pink.   It is coarse and gritty and is rarely covered with a slip.   The paint varies in color from brown to

black.   White is also frequently used for the design—a pecu-
liarity often noted of Cretan geometric vases and generally
attributed to Minoan tradition.

OBJECTS FOUND.

The objects found in 1910 at Vrokastro, arranged according to the rooms in which they occurred, will now be described.
The rooms, the numbers of which do not appear in the following lists, yielded nothing but potsherds.

ROOM 6.

Amphora, Fig. 54.   The pieces of this vase were found
in the southeast corner of the room, some of them under a col-
lapsed wall.   The vase was doubtless left in the corner of the
room at the time of the abandonment of the site.   It is made
of buff clay; the exterior, from a line on the shoulder to the
base, is covered with black paint except for a reserved panel
between the handles, which is ornamented with zigzag lines
and a row of herring-bone pattern.   The shape of the vase,
the type of double handle,[1] and the reserved panel indicate
a fully developed geometric style.

The sherds that lay below the floor level of this room,
which was in this case indicated by a column base, were principally of the late Mycenæan style.

ROOM 8.

1. Bronze fibula, Pl. XIX b, asymmetrical, an arm having
been introduced to include thick folds of drapery, but developed
beyond doubt from the fiddle-bow type of fibula.   A similar
fibula was found in Tomb 38 at Enkomi, Cyprus.[2]

---

[1] This type of handle has also an earlier history, Mackenzie, *loc. cit.*, p. 433.
[2] Murray, *Excavations at Cyprus*, p. 51 and Fig. 27.

2. Bronze disk, .03 m. diam., ornamented with two perforations and with a circle of punctuated dots. This disk lay with the fibula in the upper stratum of deposit. At the same level further to the east were parts of three animal figures like those in Fig. 56, a triton shell, and bones of animals.

Fig. 54. Amphora from Upper Stratum of Room 6 (1 : 7).

3. Parts of three badly corroded iron blades. These lay at the south end of the room together with the following.

4. Round-bodied pithos, ht. .645, whole except for a break at the rim.

5. Fragment of a fibula similar in type to that in Pl. XX B.

Room 9.

1. Clay face, Fig. 55 B, broken around the edges, from an image mounted on a cylindrical base like that of Fig. 55 A. Paint is applied to the chin, mouth, eyes, and nose.

2. Large round-bodied pithos with rope pattern around the rim.

3. Unpainted flaring bowl like that of Fig. 92.

4. Horns of an agrimi.

Room 11.

Whether this room was reached by a passageway to the west of

Fig. 55. A, Clay Figurine from Room 17; B, Face of Similar Figurine from Room 9 (1 : 3).

Rooms 9 and 10 is uncertain, for the walls here were in a ruined condition.   At the south end of room is a large boulder.   A few feet from the boulder against the east wall of Room 11 were found the objects enumerated below.

1. Terra cotta head of horse, Fig. 56 A, with bridle in painted relief.   The bridle is like a modern one, except that it has no strap under the throat.   The eyes, mouth, and forelock, as well as the bridle, are painted.

2. Horse's head, Fig. 56 B, which had served, it seems, as handle for a lid. Cf. *Mon. Ant.* VI, Pl. XII, 62.

3. Head, body, and one foot of the horse shown in Fig. 56 F. The other pieces were recovered in Room 17.

4. Unpainted flask, with one handle, and slight central protuberances, Fig. 57 E.

5. Lid with painted rays from the central knob to the rim.

Fig. 56. Clay Figurines from the Town (1 : 8).

6. Bronze disk .093 m. diam., ornamented with a central boss and row of punctuated dots around the rim, Fig. 58 H. There are four perforations in the part preserved and there must have been five originally, one in the center and four around the circumference. Similar objects were found in the Psychro Cave and called tentatively by Mr. Hogarth miniature shields.[1]

[1] *B. S. A.*, VI, p. 109, Fig. 41.

In Tomb B at Mouliana, Mr. Xanthoudides found similar but larger disks and connected them with the votive cymbals found at Olympia.[1]

7. Spear-end of hammered bronze, Fig. 59 D.   The ferrule is made by means of two cross cuttings at the shoulders, the piece cut away being then bent and hammered around the shaft.[2]

8. Spear-end of hammered bronze, Fig. 59 F.   In this specimen the transition from shoulder to ferrule is gradual; the

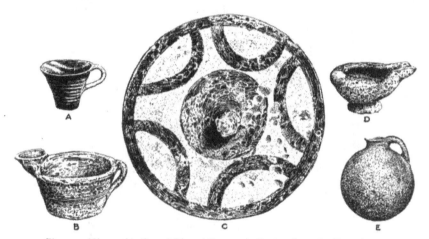

Fig. 57.   Minoan (A, C, and D) and Geometric Pottery from the Town (1 : 6).

bronze of the blade is bent without cutting and hammered around the shaft.

9. Spear-end of hammered bronze, similar to the foregoing but larger, Fig. 59 C.

10. Spear-end of cast bronze welded to iron shaft, Fig. 59 B. This specimen is of good lanceolate shape with a slight mid-

[1] 'Εφ. 'Αρχ. 1904, p. 45, Fig. 11; *Olympia Tafelband* IV, Pl. XXVI, 517.   See also Daremberg and Saglio, s. v. *cymbala*, and Arch. Anz., 1913, pp. 47-53.

[2] For a similar type, cf. Carapanos, *Dodona*, Pl. LVII, 8.

rib; the piece of iron to which it is welded is broken at the further end and has a slightly greater diameter at this end

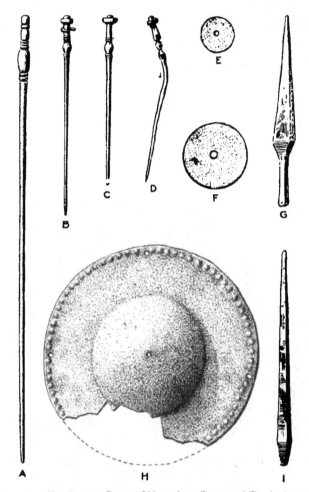

Fig. 58.   Miscellaneous Bronze Objects from Town and Tombs (2 : 3).

than where it is joined to the spear-point.   This seems to indicate that the entire shaft was made of iron.

11. Spear-end of cast bronze, Fig. 59 A, tip slightly broken.

The type is similar to that of the preceding, except that the blade is much longer and the transition from blade to shaft

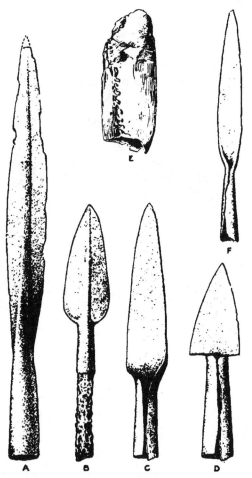

Fig. 59.   Spear-ends from Room 11 and (E) Remains of Wooden Handle with Coating of Thin Bronze Sewn with Linen Thread (1 : 2).

more gradual.   A similar spear-end was found in the graves of Mycenæ.[1]   These five bronze spear-ends lay close together

[1] 'Εφ. 'Αρχ., 1888, Pl. 9, 26.

under the east wall of the room.   Together with them were the
rotted remains of two iron spear-ends.

ROOM 12.

In the northeast corner of this room, where the rock sloped
sharply away, was a pithos containing the skull and bones of
a child.   It was inserted below the level of the floor and was
not inverted.   Inside the jar and just below the flat stone that

Fig. 60.   Vases from the Town (1 : 7).

covered it was the cup of Fig. 60 B.   It is decorated with horizontal bands and with groups of vertical lines straight and waved,
on the shoulder.

The practice of burying children in jars was usual both in
the bronze age and in the succeeding age of iron.[1]   In the
bronze age adults also were buried under inverted jars, so that
the phenomenon is not then so striking as in the later period,
when the bodies of adults were disposed of by quite different

---

[1] See *Spboungaras*, p. 73; Philios, 'Εφ. 'Αρχ., 1889, p. 186; Poulsen, *Die Dipylongräber
und die Dipylonvasen*, pp. 23-25; Dragendorff, *Thera*, II, p. 84.

methods.   The place of burial is also in this case significant; the interment is made not in a cemetery but within the walls of a house.   A parallel to this custom may now be adduced from the bronze age, for in recent excavations at Phylakopi on Melos, Mr. R. M. Dawkins found intra-mural burials which date from the closing period of the first city.

From this room came also the krater of Fig. 61.   The lower part of the vase is, save for the foot, unpainted.   The

Fig. 61.   Krater in the Quasi-Geometric Style from Room 12 (1 : 5).

upper part is painted black with a reserved panel between the shoulders, which is filled with two groups of concentric circles embellished with dots and by a central ornament made up of a parallelogram and triangles.

Room 13.

In the upper stratum of this room were found the following objects.

1. Bowl, Fig. 60 A.   This shape is one of the commonest

found on Vrokastro; its prototype appears in the Late Minoan III b period.[1] The handles are horizontal and are placed high on the shoulder. The decoration of the reserved panel consists of a series of cross-hatched lozenges.

2. Bronze fibula, Pl. XIX, 1. The thinner part of this specimen is broken; whether it belonged to the clasp or to a flat ornament in the center of a symmetrical fibula is uncertain.

3. Bronze pin, Fig. 58 C. This type corresponds closely to those found in the tombs (*ibid.* B and D).

4. Slender bronze needle.

5. Similar needle of bone.

ROOM 17.

This was one of the rooms in which the deposits of pottery had been overturned. Few sherds were found near the east wall; near the west wall, whither the rains had carried them, were fragments of geometric pottery underlying typical Late Minoan III pieces. At the south end of the room under a flimsy wall indicated by dotted lines on the plan were the objects enumerated below.

1. Clay head on columnar basis, Fig. 55 A. The workmanship is crude. A reddish paint is applied profusely to the hair, lips, eyes, and forehead. The long curls, which are plastically rendered, extended once to the bottom of the base, which is further adorned with a panel of geometric ornament.

2. Fragments of figurines of animals, including several pieces of the horse of Fig. 56 F, the legs and other parts of a similar figurine, the head of a sheep, Fig. 56 E. With these were the horns of an agrimi and a triton shell, the invariable accompaniment of figurines on Vrokastro. They indicate a shrine,

---

[1] *B. S. A.*, IX, p. 319, Fig. 19.

and in view of the fact that pieces of the same figure were recovered from different rooms, it seems likely that they come from a single shrine, the offerings at which had been thrown out into neighboring areas.

3. Fragment of heavy bar of iron, rectangular in section.[1]
4. Glass bead.
5. Fragment of iron blade.

ROOM 20.

The principal object found in this room was the bowl of Fig. 60 D. It is made of coarse, porous clay and is decorated with a simple meander painted in dull black. This bowl was found in the uppermost stratum and dates accordingly from the last period of the Vrokastro settlement. Immediately below the floor level marked by this vase were Late Mycenæan fragments, one of which is shown in Fig. 49 G; this juxtaposition of L. M. III b and geometric types may indicate that the intervening period of quasi-geometric art was short.

ROOM 21.

Three cups with broken bases from a kernos. Compare *B. S. A.* XII, p. 16, Figs. 3 and 4.

ROOM 22.

From the uppermost stratum of this room came most of the pieces of the bowl shown in Pl. XXVI. The others were found in Room 24. The clay of which this vase is made differs widely from that of the other Vrokastro specimens. It is fine and hard and its color is a dark, reddish brown. The shape,

---

[1] Cf. Körte, *Gordion*, in *Ergänzungsband* V of *Jahrbuch*, p. 79, *abb.* 69 b.

a large shallow pyxis, is a familiar type in the geometric period.[1] The lid, of which a single fragment only was recovered, was doubtless surmounted by a high handle. The decoration is applied in the compact and mathematical manner of the fully developed style of the mainland. The separate motives, especially the swastika, indicate the same period. Because of the clay and of the character of the ornament, this vase must be regarded as an importation. The sherds in the two rooms where the pieces of this vase were found were of the typical Vrokastro geometric style analogous to the vase of Fig. 60 D. We may infer, therefore, that the compact style of the mainland was contemporary with the open geometric style of Crete.

ROOM 24.

In the upper stratum of this room were found the following objects.

1. Clay scoop, ht. .07 cm. The handle of this specimen serves also as a means of support.[2]

2. Two-handled bowl with cup-like spout, Fig. 57 B.[3]

3. Lid with moulded decoration about the rim.

4. Unpainted clay dish of the shape of the vase in Fig. 60 D containing a light spongy brown mass which proved on chemical analysis to be a mixture of iron, lime, and silica with a small amount of aluminum. The iron was present in the form of limonite, lime in the form of calcite, and the silica in the form of sand composed of grains of quartz. Apparently, this was a charge for smelting, the sand having been added as a flux.

[1] Cf. e.g. Ἐφ. Ἀρχ., 1898, Pl. IV, 6.

[2] For a similar type see Xanthoudides, Ἐφ. Ἀρχ., 1904, p. 18, Fig. 2, and Hogarth, *B. S. A.* VI, p. 105.

[3] Cf. Wace and Thompson, *Prehistoric Thessaly*, p. 211, Fig. 146 c.

ROOM 25.

In a mass of débris thrown into a deep pocket in this room was found the crude model of a horse and chariot shown in Fig. 62, an imitation probably of Cypriote models.

ROOM 26.

Two well-marked deposits dating the one from the geometric, the other from the Middle Minoan period were found in this room. The level of the upper deposit was marked by the presence of whole vases. The following objects were found.

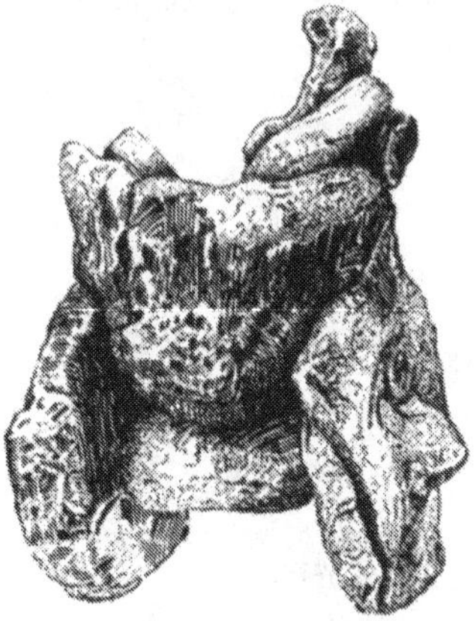

Fig. 62. Crude Model of Chariot and Charioteer from Room 25 (5 : 8).

1. Jar with panel of meander ornament, Fig. 60 C. The upper part of this vase is covered with dark paint except for a reversed panel on either shoulder on which is painted a partial meander.

2. Two clay weights in the shape of truncated pyramids.[1]

3. Head of clay figurine, Fig. 63. The lower surface shows a broken edge, the outline of which indicates that the head was once mounted on a columnar basis like that of Fig. 55 A. The face was originally covered with a slip which has been chipped off from the cheeks and along the outer edge, leaving a coarser red clay exposed beneath. The eyebrows, eyelashes, lips and chin show traces of red paint; a protruding bit of clay on the right cheek is the only remnant of the moulded curls which once bordered the face. The expression of the face achieves

---

[1] Cf. Doerpfeld, *Troia und Ilion*, p. 410, Fig. 416.

in this figure something akin to dignity and reveals far higher skill in the koroplastic art than do other figurines from the site.

4. Symmetrical beaded fibula, Pl. XX B. This fibula is of the same type as those from the bone-enclosures discussed below on p. 84.

5. Two bronze disks with central perforations, probably used as pendants, Fig. 58 E and F.[1]

6. In the lower deposit of this room above a floor of trodden earth were found the pieces of the jar in Fig. 64. It is wheel

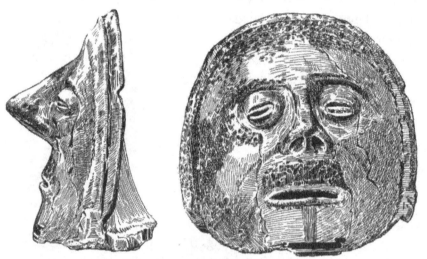

Fig. 63.   Head of Clay Figurine from Upper Stratum of Room 26 (1 : 2).

made and the clay is coarse, but because of its shape, its simple curvilinear ornament and the position where it was found, it must be assigned to the Middle Minoan period.

7. In the lower level of this room but unassociated with Minoan sherds was a child-burial in a jar. It was found in the southwest corner and belongs doubtless to the geometric period.

[1] Cf. *Argive Heraeum* II, Pl. XCIX; *British Museum Catalog of Terra-cottas*, Pl. XIV; *Mon. Ant.* VII, 239 and 241, Figs. 31 and 32.

ROOM 27.

The stratification of this room has already been described and mention has been made of the lamp of Fig. 57 D from the uppermost stratum. At a level only slightly lower than this lamp and at a distance of only a few centimeters from Late Minoan III b sherds was found a fibula of fiddle-bow type.

Fig. 64. Middle Minoan Jar from Lowest Stratum, Room 26 (1 : 6).

Pl. XIX A. This is the only fibula of this type that came to light in either town or tombs. It is generally held to be the oldest type of fibula known to the Mediterranean area; it was found in Tomb No. 8 of the lower town at Mycenæ.[1] It belongs accordingly to the Late Minoan III period. The fact that this fibula did not occur in the Zafer Papoura cemetery confirms the

[1] 'Εφ. 'Αρχ., 1888, Pl. 9, 1 and 2.

statement of p. 19, that Vrokastro takes up the tale of Cretan ceramic history where the Knossian cemetery leaves off.

The following Middle Minoan specimens were recovered from this room.

1. Cup, .07 cm. high, .096 m. diam., of brown clay, Fig. 57 A. The inside is entirely covered with brownish black paint, and is further decorated with white festoons. The outside has a broad band about the rim and another about the base. Traces remain of narrower stripes which encircled the body of the vase.

2. Jug, Pl. XXV, 1, part of spout missing. The entire surface of the vase is covered with a metallic black paint over which are splashes of white. The decoration, which presents a new phase of Minoan ornament, seems to imitate the surface of a breccia vase.

Room 30.

Veined marble bowl, ht. .05 m., diam. of mouth .046 m. As in the case of the other stone vases from Vrokastro, only a small piece of stone has been removed from the center, so that a thick wall is left. This method is characteristic of the decadent period of stone-cutting and stands in marked contrast to the skillful cutting of the delicate Early Minoan stone vases.

2. Fragments of a steatite cup.

3. Clay seal with rosette on the sealing surface, Fig. 65.

Room 36.

In the upper stratum, a veined marble bowl was found, ht. .04 m., diam. of mouth .042 m.

Near the number 36 on the plan where a wall runs at right angles to the escarpment of the rock, earth and fragments of pottery were noticed beneath the wall. The stones of the wall were accordingly removed and the following Middle Minoan pieces brought to light.

1. Part of cup, Fig. 66 A, decorated with white spirals interspersed with leaves.

2. Low, straight-sided cup, ht. .054, diam. of mouth, .082, decorated with heart-shaped motives embellished within with leaves, two of which are red and two white. The same design is also applied to the base of the cup, the interstices of the pattern being here filled with triangles.

3. Cup of similar shape, Fig. 66 B. The restoration of the design is possible from the fragments preserved; it consists of clusters of loops connected with slant-ing lines. A similar ornament decorates the base.

4. Lid, Fig. 57 C, with central knob and dec-oration of loops.

Fig. 65.
(2 : 3.)

5. Small jug with incised ornament, Fig. 67. This vase is the exact counterpart of vases found at Chamaizi (Χαμαῖζι), and published in Ἐφ. Ἀρχ., 1906, Pl. 9, 1, 2, and 3. It belongs to the Early Minoan II period and is the only specimen from Vrokastro which can be assigned to so early an epoch. The other vases from beneath this wall were associated with sherds characteristic of the Middle Minoan I period.

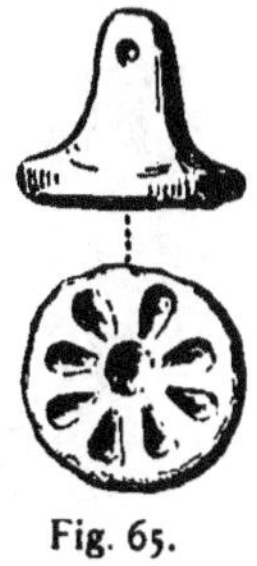

Just east of 36, on the limit of the plan, was found a small bronze saw like those found in the tombs. Further to the southeast near the crest of the hill where the soil was shallowest the workmen were in the habit of gathering for their noonday recess. They one day noticed that the inch or so of soil which here remained was packed with chips and filings of bronze. Evidently a smithy had been located here. Among the hundreds of bits found was a conical piece terminating in a hook. The workmen at once recognized it as the tip end of a distaff, the piece which holds the wool. Similar distaff ends were found by Mr. Hogarth in the Psychro Cave.[1]

The group of houses which was unearthed in 1912 yielded less than that dug in 1910. The sherds were numerous, but unbroken pieces or such as could be restored were few. No Minoan sherds were found except in fillings. Ordinarily there was only one stratum to be taken into account, that of the geometric period. Of the objects now to be enumerated from

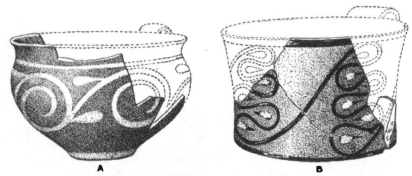

Fig. 66. Middle Minoan Cups from beneath Wall of Room 36 (2 : 3).

these houses, no two came from the same room. They will therefore be listed without regard to their finding-place.

1. Bowl of a type frequently represented by the sherds, Fig. 68 B, the handles and other pieces missing. The coarse, gritty clay has a buff color. The interior, both at the base and around the rim, has been daubed with reddish paint. Of the outside the lower half is also covered with the same. On the shoulder vertical lines divide the reserved space into two panels each decorated with a row of quirks.

2. Similar bowl, Fig. 68 C. The rim is painted within as

---

[1] B. S. A. VI, p. 112, Fig. 46.

well as without.   The interior is further decorated with a horizontal band about the shoulders.   On the outside the lower part is left undecorated; the upper part shows the usual panel decoration, the ornament consisting here of a dotted network pattern.

3. Similar bowl, Fig. 69.   The decoration which fills the panel is made up of straight lines, vertical and diagonal.

4. Jug with pour-handle and two low horizontal handles, Pl. XXVII, 3.   The neck and a part of the pour-handle is missing.   The clay is coarse and gritty and the decoration badly worn.   This vase presents close analogies to that in Fig. 99 B, from Bone-enclosure VI, and serves accordingly to connect the houses with the later type of tomb.

Fig. 67   (3 : 5).

5. Amphora, Pl. XXVIII, found in one of the upper corners of the room, the very uneven floor of which appears in Pl. XXIII. The shape is typical of the fully developed geometric style.   The clay is slightly more reddish than that usual on Vrokastro, but the difference is not enough to warrant the inference that this is an imported piece.   The decoration is confined to a small area of the vase.   Broad and narrow horizontal stripes cover almost entirely the lower portion.   A reserved panel on the neck is ornamented with a meander motive framed with lines. A second reserved panel on the shoulder is divided horizontally into three sections and filled with zigzags and dots.   The handles are ornamented with linear patterns.

6. As stated on p. 7, the walls on the north face of Vrokastro were several times tested for the purpose of ascertaining their date.   At a distance of a hundred meters or so from the

houses dug in 1912, and half-way between these houses and the point where the north face of the mountain falls away in precipitous cliffs, a cave-like recess was examined. It contained the bowl of Pl. XXIX, 2. It was inverted and below it were traces of a few bones, unburned. It was doubtless a child-burial adjacent to houses on this part of the hill. The clay is coarse and gritty, the paint a mere wash, and the decoration crude. Panels are reserved in the usual way on the shoulder and in them are painted groups of vertical lines; the intermediate spaces are cross-hatched. On either side of this decoration are curvilinear motives, the poor relic of Minoan naturalism.

Fig. 68. A, Jug; B and C, Bowls (1 : 5).

7. In the hardpan, which served as floor at one end of a large room, a circular depression had been cut within which was found a bowl containing the bones of a small animal. These bones were sent to Professor Keller of Zürich, who kindly examined them for me and declared them to be those of a rodent, and not of a domesticated animal.

8. After the discovery of the large chamber-tomb (p. 49) on Karakovilia, a search was made for more tombs in this vicinity. These were not found, but house-walls everywhere came to light. Most of these houses were blackened by fire. In one of them, that directly opposite the large chamber-tomb, was a cup which also was blackened by fire. It is made of

coarse, buff clay and is covered with black paint, save for one reserved panel opposite the handle, which is ornamented with a waved line and with a row of quirks between horizontal lines.

9. In an adjacent house south of the chamber-tomb, was found a low open dish of smooth, finely polished gray ware. The finish of the clay recalls Early Minoan II or even neolithic ware. The handles are pared into shape and contain perforations for attaching a lid. Together with the fragments of this vase were found those of a similar dish which showed a number of holes where it had been anciently mended. The rest of the

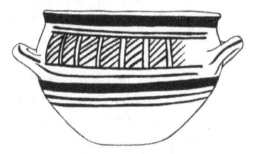

Fig. 69. Bowl from the Town.

sherds from this room were of ordinary geometric types. The entirely different character of the clay and the finish of these vases imply that they were either importations or heirlooms. A similarly shaped vase from Mirabello province is published by Mr. Droop in *B. S. A.*, XII, p. 38, Fig. 16. This specimen and the others cited in the discussion concerning it differ from ours in that their bases are decorated with a foliate ornament which is regarded by Mr. Droop as Minoan. It is not strikingly such, but it may at least be said that the decoration, like the clay and technique, must be regarded as either archaic or foreign. On the whole, this is a ware which might repay further investigation.

The objects other than pottery found in 1912 in the Vrokastro houses are as follows:

1. Four bronze rings, Fig. 70.

2. A quantity of small faience beads like the smallest beads shown in Pl. XXXV.

3. Sword of cast bronze, Pl. XXI G, the tip broken. The blade is adorned with three grooves. Two rivets are still in place and there is a hole for a third. This sword was found together with a clay disk like that in Fig. 83, and pieces of geometric bowls. In the same room were bones. It may be, accordingly, that we have here to do with a burial adjacent to a house. These objects were found in the upper level, so that they cannot represent a burial beneath the floor of a house.[1]

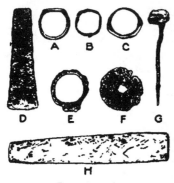

Fig. 70 (1 : 3).

4. Bronze wedge, Fig. 70 D, from the room adjoining that in which the foregoing were found.

5. Implement of soft stone, probably a whetstone, Fig. 70 H. It is too light to have served as an instrument for cutting or as a chisel. Except for the lack of perforations it resembles the whetstone from Chamber-Tomb IV.

6. Bronze needle.

7. Bronze pin with large head, Fig. 70 G.

---

[1] Since going to press there has appeared in Vol. XVIII, p. 282, of the Annual of the British School at Athens an article by Mr. T. E. Peet in regard to similar sword-blades found in Egypt. One of these bears the cartouche of Seti II and dates from the last of the thirteenth century B. C. This date is considerably earlier than that to which the Vrokastro sword is assigned, but it is to be noted first, that the sword bearing the cartouche of Seti II is not certainly of the same type as that reproduced by Mr. Peet and secondly, that, as he himself suggests, it is a type that "may have been current for many years".

8. Bronze figurine with arms upraised, Fig. 71. This figurine is the only specimen of the kind found on Vrokastro: the

position of the upraised arms is interesting because of its resemblance to the attitudes of Late Minoan terra-cotta figurines.

9. Sealstone of steatite, Fig. 72, found near the surface. No sherds lay close at hand, but those at the same level some distance away were of the geometric period. The ornament on the sealing surface is a highly conventionalized squid.[1]

Fig. 71 (2 : 3).

In enumerating the objects from the Vrokastro houses there should not be left out of account the humbler objects for domestic use. Among these were a saddle quern, several stone polishers, and whetstones of various shapes. The material for the latter was probably quarried at Elouda ('Ελοῦντα), a place which today furnishes whetstones for the islanders. At a low level in one room a green steatite celt came to light, a survival of the Early Minoan period. Quadrangular blocks of stone containing a central depression were frequently noted; the workmen ventured the explanation that they had been used in spinning to support and keep in a constant position the end of the spindle. Whorls for spindles were also found. These are shown in Fig. 73, together with perforated pieces of steatite and clay beads which were evidently used as ornaments. These crude ornaments were indeed so numerous as to be one of the characteristic features of a geometric deposit,

Fig. 72 (3 : 4).

---

[1] For Late Minoan seals in geometric surroundings, cf. B. S. A. VIII, p. 270.

and might well serve to identify any Cretan site of this period.[1]
The oblong piece of steatite ornamented with dots and irregular lines was purchased of a man who found it on the
lower slopes of Vrokastro.

Fig. 73   Spindle-whorls and Ornaments of Clay and Steatite from the Town (1 : 2).

[1] Cf. *A. J. A.*, 1901, p. 282, Fig. 8.

THE TOMBS.

In addition to the burials of children beneath the floors of houses, four types of interments were found in the vicinity of Vrokastro. They were: chamber-tombs (7), bone-enclosures (12), pithos-burials (4), and a single interment underneath an overhanging rock.

The chamber-tombs were sunk, as already stated, in the white chalky soil known as kouskoura, an exceedingly hard subsoil, and were lined with rubble masonry. In no case was a roof intact, but the uppermost course showed in several instances an inward projection. In Fig. 74 is shown a diagrammatic plan of Tomb I on Karakovilia, which, although it was both larger and more regularly constructed than the others, is yet typical. Details of construction will be given for each tomb.

CHAMBER-TOMB I ON KARAKOVILIA.

The dimensions of this tomb may be seen from the diagram. Against the wall opposite the dromos was found a circular stone, in the neighborhood of which most of the bones and fragments of vases were found. It apparently had served as a table of offerings.[1] The disturbed condition of the tomb, however, does not warrant positive statements. It will be seen from the appended lists that thirty-three vases with many more cups were recovered from this tomb. Of these only four or five, those which had been inserted in other vases and two or three cups, were intact; the others had to be pieced

[1] Cf. *B. S. A.* VI, p. 83.

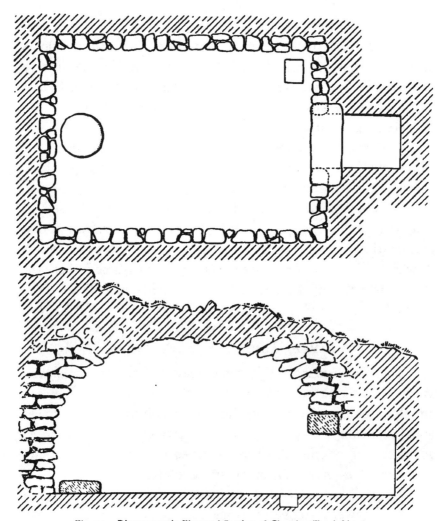

Fig. 74.   Diagrammatic Plan and Section of Chamber Tomb No. 1.

METER.

together from countless fragments.   As a result of heavy rains
or of other natural processes, both bones and vase-fragments
had worked their way through the soil to a considerable
distance from their original position; some pieces of the vase
of Pl. XXX were found at a height of .65 m. from the floor
of the tomb, others on the floor itself.   Pieces of the tripod of
Fig. 80 were recovered from the four corners of the tomb.
Almost all the pieces of the various objects found in the tomb
were, however, eventually recovered.

The floor of the tomb had evidently been strewn with
sand and river-pebbles, for these were found in abundance.
In the northeast corner was a rectangular depression, .26 m.
long, .22 m. broad, and .15 m. deep.   Nothing but a few
potsherds was found within it.   It may have been used for
libations.[1]

The bones recovered from this tomb were in a very fragmentary condition.   Most of them showed indisputable traces
of burning, some bits being actually burned to charcoal.   In at
least two cases the burned bones had been buried within jars.[2]
In other cases the bones were interred outside jars; whether
all of these had been burned or not was difficult to determine
because of their rotted condition.   They were found in a small
heap, which indicates that the body was at least not stretched
out to its full length.   One child's skull was found which it was
plain to see had not been burned; evidently the bodies of
children who were buried within tombs were also an exception
to the practice of cremation.   It was estimated that at least
six interments had been made within this tomb.

---

[1] A comparable pit was found in Tomb A at Mouliana, Ἐφ.Ἀρχ., 1904, p. 24, Fig. 5. It
was, however, of a different shape.

[2] One of these jars is shown in Fig. 77; the other was a coarse, unpainted jar and is not
shown.

The vases from this tomb are as follows.

1. Large straight-sided jar, Pl. XXX, of soft yellowish clay. The decoration, which is badly worn, is divided into narrow vertical panels which are filled with simple linear motives and

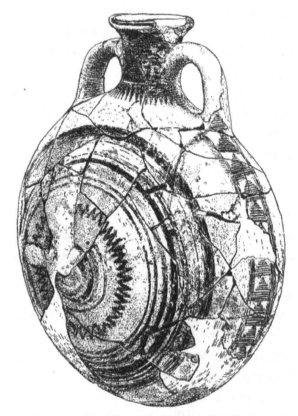

Fig. 75.   Flask of the Quasi-Geometric Style from Chamber-Tomb 1 (1 : 4).

with the triangles characteristic of an early stage of Cretan geometric art.[1] The handles are curious; they are flat and are applied to the outer surface of the vase from the rim nearly

---

[1] For the use of triangles in this period compare Wide, *Athen. Mitt.* XXXV, p. 21, and Pl. VI, 2.

to the base.[1]   The fragments of this jar were found scattered throughout the tomb; whether it originally contained human remains is accordingly uncertain.

2. Large flask, Fig. 75, of soft yellow clay.   The design, which is badly worn, consists on either face of the flask of concentric circles, broken once by a circle of zigzag lines.[2]   The neck is entirely covered with black paint, below which is a fringe of vertical lines.   Around the outside of the vase from handle to handle runs a chain of triangles.   The pieces of this extraordinarily large flask, which measures no less than .455 m. in height and .37 m. in diameter, were found scattered throughout the tomb.

3. Open-work vase of soft buff clay, Pl. XXXI, 2.   The horizontal parts of the vase and the perforated quadrangular pieces were once covered with a reddish brown paint, of which little now remains.   The slanting pieces of the lower part seem to have been unpainted.   The openings of the vase were apparently cut when the vase was partially hardened.   Such open-work vases, useful for holding fruit or the like, are common in the geometric period,[3] but have not been found before in Crete.

4. Open-work vase similar to the foregoing except that the pattern in both upper and lower courses is the same, Pl. XXXI, 1.   Only the horizontal pieces were painted.

5. Bowl and cover, Pl. XXXII, 2, of soft buff clay.   The design on the shoulder, painted in dull brown, consists of groups of vertical lines and rows of short slanting lines.   Intervening panels are adorned with a single horizontal waved line.   The

---

[1] For similar handles, cf. the jar from Erganos, *A. J. A.*, 1901, Pl. VI, 4.

[2] Cf. Wide, *loc. cit.*, p. 28 and Pl. 5, 2.

[3] Cf. Dragendorff, *Thera* II, p. 151, *Abb.* 363 and 364; *id.*, p. 308, *Abb.* 495; *Annali del Instituto*, Vol. 44, 1872, *Tav. d'agg.* K 12; *Jahrbuch*, 1888, p. 341. Fig. 23; *Athen. Mitt.*, 1893, Pl. VIII, 4; Ἐφ. Ἀρχ., I, 1898, p. 107, Fig. 27.

lower parts of the vase and the lid are decorated with bands; the handles are also decorated with horizontal stripes. The lid has two perforations by which it was tied to the handle.

6. Similar amphora and cover, Pl. XXXII, 1. The clay is the same as in the preceding; the paint is redder. The lids and lower parts of the vases correspond exactly. The decoration on the shoulder here consists of horizontal rows of triangles, those in the second row being differently set from the others.

Fig. 76.   Krater of the Quasi-Geometric Style from Chamber-Tomb I (1 : 6).

7. Krater, Fig. 76, of good buff clay. The interior is covered with black paint. On the outside the decoration consists of horizontal bands and of the pattern described on p. 21. The handles are of a double type frequent in the geometric period.

8. Large jar which contained vase 26, and burned bones inside, Fig. 77. The clay is reddish buff; the decoration consists of horizontal bands and on the shoulder of groups of vertical lines, the outermost of which are fringed.

9. Kylix of fine buff clay and good hard slip, Pl. XXV, 2. The design is painted in reddish brown and consists of horizontal

bands, a row of lozenges on the shoulder, and another of triangles on the foot.   The interior is covered with dark paint.
The handles are embellished with knobs.

10. Bowl of gritty buff clay.   The inside is covered with a
thin black paint.   The color of the paint on the outside shades
from brown to red.   The pattern resembles that of 5.

11. Similar bowl of fine buff clay with slip, Pl. XXIX, 1.
Part of the foot and several other pieces are missing.   The

Fig. 77.   Krater from Chamber-Tomb I (1 : 6).

paint used for the interior and for the design shades from brown
to black.   The decoration presents a new combination of familiar
motives; it resembles that of Pl. XXXII, 2, but has in addition
the quasi-Minoan curl which appeared on the vase on Pl.
XXIX, 2.

12–17. Similar smaller bowls, Fig. 78.   The clay of which
they are made is light, thin, and well sifted.   The interior as
heretofore is covered with dark paint.   The design consists
merely of horizontal bands and groups of vertical lines.

18. Similar bowl, the decoration of which was achieved by dipping the vase as far as the foot into dark paint. This bowl together with the preceding numbers 10–17 are, as regards shape, merely enlargements of the following.

19–22. Cups, decorated like the above by being dipped into black paint, Fig. 79. Four specimens were nearly intact. It was estimated that 33 had originally been interred in the tomb. These cups abound on every Cretan geometric site. They were found by Mr. Hogarth in the geometric graves at

Fig. 78.   Bowl from Chamber-Tomb I (1 : 3).

Knossos;[1] by Mrs. Hawes at Kavousi;[2] by Sig. Halbherr at Erganos; and lately in great numbers by Mr. Hagidakis in the upper stratum at Tylissos. They have also been found in Thessaly.[3]

23. Pieces of an oinochoe, of soft yellow clay with high slim neck and twisted handle. The entire vase was covered with a reddish paint. The clay of this specimen was only partially baked and consequently crumbled to bits.

[1] B. S. A. VI, p. 84, Fig. 26.
[2] A. J. A., 1901, Pl. I (opp. 124).
[3] Wace and Thompson, *Prehistoric Thessaly*, p. 209 c.

24. Upper part of flaring bowl of good buff clay.   The design painted in brown consists of groups of vertical and slanting lines, the outermost fringed.   The shape of the rim indicates that the bowl once had a cover.

25. Amphora, Pl. XXXIII, of buff clay.   Pieces from the rim were not recovered.   The lower part of the vase is decorated with two broad and two narrow bands of reddish paint.   On the shoulder are groups of concentric half-circles within the innermost of which is what looks to be a survival of a Late Minoan III stereotyped bud.[1]   Waved lines ornament the neck and appear also in the decoration of the shoulder.

26. Amphora of fine buff clay orna-  mented with horizontal bands and with a single zigzag line on the shoulder.   The shape with its slender foot and narrow neck is in marked contrast to the preceding amphora. This specimen was found intact together with burned bones within the jar of Fig. 77.

Fig. 79 (1 : 5).

27–28. Pieces of two flasks similar to that of Fig. 95, but smaller.   One has an air vent bored through the base of the handle.

29. Small cup of buff clay, part of rim lacking.   The decoration in dark paint is confined to two horizontal stripes and to a row of vertical lines about the shoulder.   This cup was found, together with the pieces of twelve iron blades, in an unpainted jar of coarse clay.

30–32. Unpainted bowl of fine buff clay.   The shape is unusually graceful and well fashioned.   It terminates below in a point as do the covers to the vases in Pl. XXXII.   The

---

[1] Cf. *Transactions of the Department of Archæology of the University of Pennsylvania,* Vol. II, Part I, p. 39, Fig. 53.

handles, which are nearly cylindrical, are attached horizontally just below the rim.   Pieces of two other similar bowls were also recovered.

33. Bügelkanne of fine buff clay with slip.   This was the only bügelkanne from the tomb.   It resembles closely that shown in Pl. XXVII, 1.   Like the other specimens from Vrokastro, it has an air-hole on the shoulder opposite the spout, and a small knob on the top of the false neck, both characteristic of post-Mycenæan bügelkannen.[1]   The decoration consists of horizontal bands and of various combinations of zigzag lines.

The objects other than pottery from this tomb were as follows.

1. Bronze tripod support, ht. 377 m., Fig. 80 and Pl. XXXIV, 1.   The fragments of this tripod were found scattered throughout the tomb.   All were recovered except a part of one leg and portions of the cross supports.   No traces were found, however, of a bowl or cauldron which surmounted it.   The tripod is made of cast bronze.   It consists of a circular support resting on three legs ornamented with lateral ridges and midribs which terminate at the top in scrolls like those on early Ionic capitals.   Above the scrolls is a low abacus.   The legs are flat except for a rounded piece above the circular foot; they are strengthened by slanting supports which pass from a point at a third of the distance of their height to the circular top, and by horizontal braces which are united in a central ring.

This tripod is in type quite similar to one found by Mr. Hogarth in Grave 3 of the geometric cemetery of Knossos, Pl. XXXIV, 2, where it was associated with a fully developed

---

[1] Cf. Wide, *Athen. Mitt.*, XXXV, p. 19; and *Jahrbuch*, 1899, p. 41, Fig. 26; Xanthoudides, 'Εφ. 'Αρχ., 1904, p. 44.

style of geometric pottery.[1]　The chief difference is in size, that from Knossos being only half as high as our specimen; there is also this difference, that the midrib on the legs of the Vrokastro tripod divides and follows the curves of the volutes,

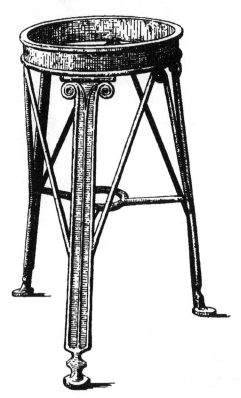

Fig. 80.　Restoration of Bronze Tripod from Chamber-Tomb I (1 : 4).

whereas that of the Knossos specimen extends straight to the abacus.

Another striking parallel to this tripod may be adduced from Cyprus.　In Grave 58 at Enkomi, were found the pieces

[1] See *B. S. A.* VI, p. 83, Fig. 25.　Mr. Hogarth has generously allowed me to reproduce this specimen here.

of a tripod now in the British Museum and reproduced here,
Pl. XXXIV, 3, by kind permission of Mr. A. H. Smith. It is
slightly taller than our specimen[1] and the circular support is
decorated with rows of herring-bone ornaments. The abacus
is lacking and the midrib of the legs runs straight to the top
as in the Knossos specimen. It also apparently once had
horizontal supports uniting in a central ring. This Enkomi
tripod was found with iron blades, an ivory draught-box, and
native Cypriote ware.[2] Another tripod similar in type but
bearing on its circular support a frieze of running animals, was
found at Curium by Cesnola, and is now in the Metropolitan
Museum.[3]

And lastly may be cited for purposes of comparison, a
tripod found in a geometric grave southwest of the Pnyx.[4]
It is .45 m. high. The legs are ornamented with herring-bone
ornament, the circular top with a row of spirals, between bands
of rope pattern.[5]

In spite of differences in ornamentation, these tripods
correspond closely in form and must date from approximately
the same period. In determining this period, the Mycenæan
character of the Curium tripod and the geometric associations
of the Knossos and the Athens specimens are important; the
former indicate the end of the Mycenæan period, the latter the

---

[1] Both Mr. Hogarth and Dr. Poulsen wrongly suppose that this Enkomi specimen is of
much smaller dimensions; the latter (*Jahrbuch* XXVI, p. 229) calls it a "Miniaturdreifuss."
In reality it is .43 m. high.

[2] See Murray, *Excavations in Cyprus*, p. 31. See also, *B. S A.* XVIII, p. 95.

[3] See Cesnola, *Cyprus, Its Cities and Tombs*, p. 335; Furtwängler, *Sitzungsberichte der bayern
Akad.*, 1905, p. 270.

[4] *Athen. Mitt.*, 1893, p. 414, Pl. XIV.

[5] The statement of Dr. Poulsen, *loc. cit.*, that the Enkomi tripod resembles this Dipylon
specimen "*bis in die kleinsten Details*" is obviously an exaggeration. With these tripods should
also be compared the fragment from the Acropolis, De Ridder, *Bronzes trouvées sur l'acropole
d'Athènes*, p. 23, Fig. 24. For the further development of this form of tripod support, compare
Mon. Ant. VII, pp. 290–326.

period of the fully developed geometric style.   Since, however, the Mycenæan style lived on late in Cyprus, the Curium specimen need not be assigned to a period earlier than that known as "sub-Mycenæan" and since, on the other hand, such pieces of bronze-work would doubtless survive for several generations, the Athens specimen and that from Knossos may well have been made, not in the period of a mature geometric style to which the pottery found with them belonged, but in an earlier period of the iron age.   We thus arrive at the conclusion that these tripods date from the sub-Mycenæan or early geometric period.   To substitute for these general terms specific dates, is difficult.   One piece of archæological evidence, however, is available in the connection established by Furtwängler between a group of Cypriote bronzes and the bronze paraphernalia made for King Solomon's temple by Hiram of Tyre.[1]   He pointed out that a bronze cart found at Larnaka, Cyprus, corresponded exactly to the description in 2 Kings, VII, 27–37, of the mekônôth made by Hiram.   Another similar cart was found in Grave 97, Enkomi.   Both specimens present such striking analogies to the tripods described both as regards technique and ornamentation that it is plausible to regard them all as the products of a single Cypriote foundry.   Furtwängler assigned the Enkomi tripod to *ca.* 1000 B. C. and the Athens specimen to the following century.[2]

2. Six faience seals, all intact but one which is broken along its shorter diameter, Fig. 81 and Pl. XXXV.   The faience of which they are made is now rotted and friable.   No traces of

---

[1] *Sitzungsberichte der bayern. Akad. der Wissenschaften*, 1899, Part II, p. 420–433. Cf. also Stade, *Zeitschrift für die alttestamentliche Wissenschaft*, 1901, Vol. XXI, p. 145, and G. Karo, *Archiv. für Religionswissenschaft*, VIII, Beiheft, pp. 54–65.

[2] Poulsen, *loc. cit.*, pp. 228 and 247, endorses this date, assigning this tripod to a period slightly anterior to 1000 B. C.

blue coloring remain; these were abundant, however, on the beads which were found with the seals and were doubtless worn with them.   The backs of the seals consist each of a pair of shells between which is a perforation.   The sealing surfaces bear in intaglio pseudo-hieroglyphs, three being like that of Fig. 81, 2, and two like that of Fig. 81, 3.   The sixth shows a hawk-like figure, Horus (?) with a staff in his hand.   The hieroglyphs, which are crudely moulded, are unintelligible.

    The question arises as to whether they are importations from Egypt, or native Cretan imitations of con-

Fig. 81.   (2 : 3)

temporary Egyptian products.   Mr. H. R. Hall, of the British Museum, adheres to the former view; Mr. Petrie suggests to me that they were made by Greeks in Egypt for export.   In view of the active commerce between Egypt and the Ægean in this era this view seems more probable than the supposition that Cretans had established native factories for the manufacture of glazed objects.

A similar seal was found in Eleutherna, Crete,[1] and another in Grave 24, Enkomi, Cyprus.[2]   Nothing is known about the associations of the Eleutherna seal; the Enkomi specimen was associated with pieces of an ivory relief and with two steatite seals the date of which could not be definitely established.   In Egypt similar seals have lately been found in the excavation of a village at Lisht which has been dated to the XX–XXII dynasties,[3] and this seems as close a date as can be assigned to them independently.

3. Beads, Pl. XXXV.   About 250 beads were recovered

[1] 'Εφ. 'Αρχ., 1907, Pl. 6, No. 42.
[2] Murray, *Excavations in Cyprus*, p. 21 and Pl. 24.
[3] I owe this information to Mr. A. M. Lythgoe, of the Metropolitan Museum.

from this tomb.   Several were of carnelian, one was of steatite, the rest of faience.   In the case of these beads it was possible to examine their material more closely than that of the seals. Some specimens were made of a grayish brown clay and almost all traces of a glaze had disappeared; others were made of a whitish clay like that of the seals and retained still their coating of pale blue glaze.   The beads of the grayish brown clay were invariably of the plain elongated type.   The others were of three types: a barrel-shaped ribbed bead, a spherical ribbed bead, and a small disk-like bead used seemingly to separate the others in stringing.   The spherical ribbed bead occurred at Amathus, Cyprus, a site which yielded scarabs of the XIX–XXI dynasties; it was found also in the Lisht villages of the XX and XXI dynasties.

4. Bronze fibula, Pl. XX C.   This fibula is asymmetrical with a high forearm separating the bow from the catch.   The arch is adorned with two bead-like protuberances.   It corresponds accordingly to the third type of fibula enumerated in Mr. J. L. Myres' classification of Cypriote fibulæ.[1]   In Cyprus it was found associated with Late Mycenæan and sub-Mycenæan pottery,[2] but there is reason to believe that it has also been found in later contexts; the record in regard to Tomb 98 at Kurion is not quite clear, and if we are not mistaken as to the type of fibula shown in Dussaud, *L'île de Chypre*, p. 207, Fig. 92, we have here an instance of its association with pottery of the Græco-Phœnician type.   This type of fibula was found at Assarlik again in sub-Mycenæan context[3] and at Aigina.[4]

5. Pieces of a bronze fibula similar to the foregoing.

[1] *Annals of Archæology and Anthropology*, Vol. III, pp. 138–144.
[2] Myres, *loc. cit.*, and Murray, *op. cit.*, p. 68 and Figs. 92 and 93.
[3] *J. H. S.* VIII, p. 74, Figs. 17 and 18.
[4] *Aigina*, Pl. 116, No. 14.

6. Larger bronze fibula of the same type as 4, except that the catch is in this case narrower at the base.   This specimen is broken into four pieces but is complete save for the tip of the pin and a bit of the clasp.

7. Pair of bronze tweezers or snuffers.

8. Gold ring with plain bezel comparable to that found in Tomb A at Mouliana.[1]   Fig. 82.

9. Bronze fish-hook.

10. Axe-head of iron, length .22 m., weight 2.475 kilograms.   Like the other objects made of iron, this axe-head is so badly corroded as to have lost its original contours.   One of the cutting edges is also broken.   The central hole for insertion of a handle is now partly choked with corroded iron and measures

Fig. 82 (3 : 5).

but .03 m. in diameter.   Originally it cannot have measured more than .04 m., which seems a very small aperture for so heavy an implement.   A carefully selected piece of wood, however, might have withstood the strain.

11. Iron adze, badly corroded.

12. Iron spear-end, Pl. XXI B.

13. Curved iron knife with short shaft for insertion in handle, Pl. XXI J.   The concave edge is for cutting.

14. Pieces of slender iron knife, length .131 m., greatest width .012 m.

15. Part of iron wedge or chisel.

In addition to these iron instruments, which were fairly well preserved, there were also found masses of corroded iron, the fragmentary remains of spear-ends, knives, and swords. Mention has already been made of the bits of twelve iron blades

---

[1] 'Εφ. 'Αρχ., 1904, p. 37, Fig. 8; cf. also a ring from Praisos, B. S. A. VIII, p. 248, Fig. 16.

found together with a cup inside a burial jar. One of these, it was noted, had bronze rivets. As many as twenty-five iron weapons, it was estimated, had been buried in the tomb. And lastly, in the enumeration of the contents of this tomb should be mentioned four large disks of clay and one of stone, Fig. 83. Three had rounded tops and resembled great loaves of bread; others were flat and one was perforated. Had such disks not been found also in the town, they might have been regarded as substitute loaves for the use of the dead. Since,

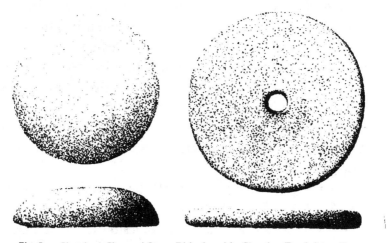

Fig. 83.   Sketch of Clay and Stone Disks found in Chamber-Tomb I (1 : 6).

however, they appeared also in the Vrokastro houses, it is preferable to regard them as heavy lids employed to cover and protect the jars in which the ashes of the dead had been laid away.

CHAMBER-TOMB II.

This tomb lies about a kilometer southwest of the Karako-vilia tomb on the west side of the ridge Mazikhortia. The chamber itself is an irregular rectangle measuring 2.04 m. from the beginning of the dromos to the rear wall and 1.70 m. in the opposite direction.   The height of the tomb as far as the upper-most course preserved was 1.09 m.   The roof had fallen in.   The dromos was .47 m. wide; its entire length was not cleared.

The contents of this tomb were extraordinary; they consisted of twenty-four skeletons, three vases and one fibula.   No traces of cremation were detected.   The space in the tomb seems scant for so many uncremated bodies, but it must be remembered that the skeletons were placed in a crouching position.   The skulls were found ranged in rows around the outside of the tomb.   The only one which was well enough preserved to be measured showed a maximum length of .187 m. and a maximum breadth of .123 m.   This specimen, however, was crushed behind the ears and somewhat flattened behind. In addition to the masses of human bones, there were also found, and these in the upper stratum of the tomb, the teeth and bones of cattle, indicating, perhaps, that a victim was slain in honor of this strange interment, which must have been due to either war or pestilence.

The meagre offerings left with these dead were as follows.

1. Small jug, Fig. 68 A, decorated with groups of horizontal lines and with a row of concentric circles on the shoulder.   This jug is the prototype of those of Fig. 97.   Similar jugs were found at Kavousi and Milatos.

2. Fragments from a bird-shaped vase like that of Fig. 92, 1.

3. Pieces of a badly rotted cup with two vertical handles and a single broad band about the body of the vase.

4. Iron fibula, Pl. XIX D, with high symmetrical arch. This *fibula ad arco*, or semicircular fibula, is found over a wide area.[1]

---

[1] For a similar specimen from Crete, see *A. J. A.*, 1901, p. 136, Fig. 2.   Outside of Crete it has been found at Ephesus (Hogarth, *Ephesus*, Pl. XVII, Nos. 12 and 13), in Italy (Montelius, *La civilisation primitive en Italie*, Serie A, Pl. V, 41; *id.*, Serie B, Pl. 213, No. 1), and in the Caucasus (Virchow, *Das Gräberfeld von Koban*, Pl. I, 4).

CHAMBER-TOMB III.

This tomb was the second found on Mazikhortia; it lies between the Karakovilia tomb and that just described. It measures 1.76 m. from the dromos to the rear wall, and 1.34 m. in the opposite direction, and was 1.36 m. deep from the floor to the uppermost course preserved. The dromos was .60 m. wide; it was faced with rubble walls to a distance of 1.51 m. The height of the dromos door was .85 m.

Seven skulls were counted in this tomb. Neither these skulls nor any other bones showed traces of burning. There was noted, however, adjacent to vases 4, 5, and 6, a few bits of charcoal, so that it is possible that these vases should be associated with a cremated interment. The presence of a quantity of beach pebbles indicated that the floor of the tomb had been prepared with these as in Chamber-Tomb I. The pottery from this tomb was as follows.

1. Small oinochoe of soft yellow clay. On the shoulder, which is sharply differentiated from the neck, is a row of concentric semicircles painted in black. Cf. Wace and Thompson, *Prehistoric Thessaly*, p. 211, Fig. 146 b.

2. Larger oinochoe, Pl. XXVII, 4, of similar but harder clay. The shape is both graceful and substantial. The design, painted in black, consists of broad bands about the body of the vase and a row of concentric circles on the shoulder. The rim, the base of the neck, and the handles are also decorated with bands. The circles have the look of being drawn with compasses. Only the upper halves of them originally showed above the top band.

3. Unpainted flask of coarse red clay, ht. .28 m.

4. Bowl and cover of finely levigated red clay without slip, Pl. XXVII, 2. The cover is slightly broken and there is

also a piece lacking from the rim.   There are holes in both cover and rim for tying.   The design, like those on vases from Chamber-Tomb I, produces a maximum of effect with a minimum of originality.   Between two horizontal bands is painted a row of lozenges, the central one filled with checkers, the outer two with cross-hatchings.   The latter show also a fringe of parallel lines like that in Pl. XXXII, 2.   A similar bowl and cover were found by Mr. Hogarth in Grave 6 of the geometric cemetery at Knossos.[1]

5. Hydria of coarse brown clay, ht. 171 m.   The pour-handle is broken away and fragments from the rim are lacking. Traces of bands of black paint remain on the shoulder and the foot.

6. Bowl with two horizontal handles.   The decoration is confined to two horizontal bands and a waved line on the shoulder.

7. Bowl with vertical handles, of soft buff clay.   The neck is ornamented with a painted zigzag pattern and the shoulder with an incised pattern of lines and dots.

8. Amphora, Fig. 84, of poor buff clay.   Several pieces are lacking.   The shape is characteristic of the mature geometric style.   Bands of black are painted on the rim, handles, the line where the neck joins the shoulder, the body of the vase, and the foot.   The main decoration on the shoulder consists of three groups of concentric circles, one partly concealed by a band of black and a hatched triangle.   Cf. *Jahrbuch*, 1899, p. 40, Fig. 22.

9. Pieces of two cups like those of Fig. 79 and pieces of a bügelkanne.

[1] *B. S. A.* VI, p. 84, Fig. 26

The objects other than pottery from this tomb were the following:

1. Bronze disk with two perforations near margin, Fig. 85 N.

2. Piece of bronze saw, perforated at one end and decorated with two lines of punctuated dots.[1]

3. Bit of yellow steatite perforated.

4. Two pendants of rock crystal, Fig. 85, O and R.

5. Faience beads, five of the small disk type, and one of the elongated type with plain surface. These are entirely similar to the beads from Chamber-Tomb I.

6. Bronze bead.

7. Small globular bead of steatite.

8. Pieces, still adhering to the knuckle bones, of two bronze rings made of flat bands.

9. Larger bronze ring, Fig. 85 A.

10. Bronze bracelet of light wire, Fig. 85 E. The bracelet is open; one tip is lacking.

11. Bronze fibula, Fig. 85 M and Pl. XX F. The type resembles that

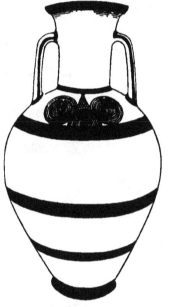

Fig. 84. Amphora (1 : 7).

of Pl. XX D but the catch is broader, the swelling on the bow larger and the bead-like ornaments of the bow are in group of threes. This specimen is only slightly asymmetrical.

12. Bronze fibula of symmetrical semicircular type, Fig. 85 Q.

---

[1] Cf. Ἐφ. Ἀρχ, 1904, p. 31; B. S. A. VII, p. 135, Fig. 46.

13. Pieces of nine straight pins their heads adorned with bosses, Fig. 85, G–L. These pins, it is now known, were used to fasten garments at the shoulder. For a discussion of the method of wearing them and of their history, see Thiersch in *Aigina*, pp. 404–410.

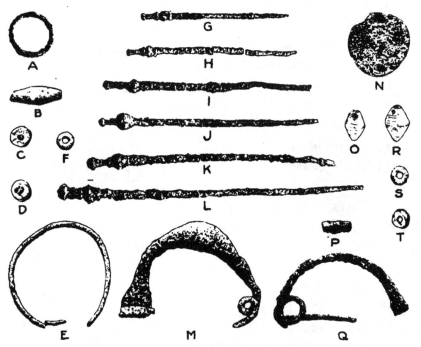

Fig. 85. Miscellaneous Small Objects from Chamber-Tomb III.

CHAMBER-TOMB IV ON AMIGTHALI.

This tomb was more irregular in shape than those just described. It is further distinguished from the others by the fact that the lintel consisted of two large stones 1.44 m. in length, .40 m. in height, and .30 m. in breadth. The greatest length of the chamber itself is 1.80 m., width 1.545 m., height as far as preserved, 1.15 m. The entire roof had fallen. Cremation, not inhumation, was practiced in this tomb.   At the right of the dromos door were the remains of a large unpainted jar of coarse clay containing a skull and bones that showed clear traces of burning.   In a bügelkanne, the side of which was broken away, there were also found burned bones, but this may have been due to chance.   Bits of bones, however, were noted in another small unpainted jug, .18 m. high.   Bones which showed signs of cremation were also found scattered about in the tomb.   Of inhumation without cremation there were no traces, although it should be stated that the difference is slight between the bones of unburned bodies and those of bodies the flesh of which has been burned away.   In cases where bones of cremated bodies were not gathered into vases, their appearance might be quite similar to that of the bones of unburned bodies the original position of which had been disturbed by the collapse of a roof.

Unfortunately the pottery from this tomb was of a very indeterminate character.   The majority of these vases were entirely unpainted.   Many were of a coarse clay which had rotted to mud before the tomb was opened.   Most of them lay opposite the door; those which could be preserved were as follows.

1. Oinochoe of coarse greenish clay, ht. .18 m., Fig. 86 E. The decoration consists of horizontal bands and of a group of narrower vertical bands below the spout, connected by slanting lines.   The shape is good and the decoration, in spite of its simplicity, effective.

2. Unpainted bowl of pinkish clay, ht. .09 m., diam. .177 m. The shape seems to be modeled after that of stone vases, Fig. 86 G.

3. Krater with horizontal handles, ht. .151 m. Piece from

the rim is lacking.   Black stripes are painted around the body
of the vase and zigzag pattern on the shoulder,[1] Fig. 86 D.

4. Triple vase of coarse red clay, Fig. 86 F.   This very
unusual vase is made up of three cups to each of which a leg
and handle are attached; one handle is missing.[2]

5. Unpainted bügelkanne, ht. 152 m., Fig. 88 C.

6. Pieces of two other bügelkannen.

Fig. 86.   Pottery from Chamber-Tomb IV (2 : 9).

7. Small cup with flaring sides and two horizontal handles,
ht. .067 m., diam. .107 m., Fig. 86 A.

8. Small bowl, Fig. 86 B, decorated with horizontal and
vertical bands.

---

[1] This vase may be compared to one found in a grave at Rakhmani, Thessaly. Wace and
Thompson, *Prebistoric Thessaly*, p. 47, Fig. 23 e.

[2] The vase at the right of Fig. 26, *B. S. A.* VI, p. 84, from Knossos cemetery, Tomb 6, is
apparently analogous. Cf. also Furtwängler and Löschcke, *op. cit.*, Pl. III, 23, VII.

The other objects found in this tomb were as follows.

1. Bronze pin, Fig. 87 K.

2. Perforated steatite disk ornamented with crudely incised design of animals, Fig. 87 G.

3. Similar undecorated disk.

4. Heavy bronze ring, Fig. 87 C.

5. Two slender bronze rings, adhering to one another, .018 m. diam.

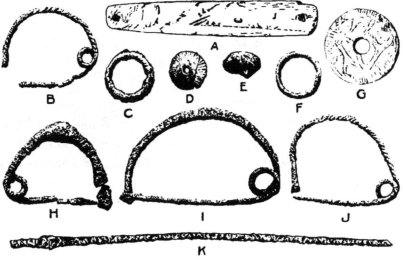

Fig. 87.　Miscellaneous Small Objects from Chamber-Tomb IV (1 : 2).

6. Whetstone, quadrangular and tapering, with string holes at either end,[1] Fig. 87 A.

7. Part of amygdaloid carnelian sealstone. The design indicates the last stages of Minoan glyptic art. Either the sealstone itself or else the stereotyped design survived from the preceding era, Figs. 87 E and 88.

Fig. 88.
Sealstone
(2 : 3.)

---

[1] Cf. Myres-Richter, *Cyprus Museum Catalog*, p. 52, 481-487.

8. Porcelain ribbed bead, Fig. 87 D. This type of bead which was conspicuous by its absence in Chamber-Tomb I, enjoyed a wide popularity in the Late Mycenæan period. It was found at Mycenæ, at Palaiokastro, and in the Zafer Papoura cemetery,[1] and lately by Mr. Stais at Sounion.

9. Eight beads of the small disk-like type like those in Fig. 85.

10. Faience seal like that of Fig. 81, 2, but slightly smaller, Pl. XXXV, upper right hand seal.

11. Globular bead of iridescent glass. Glass, it is now known, makes its appearance at the end of the Minoan age. It was found, for example, in the Zafer Papoura tombs, *op. cit.*, p. 72.

12. Cylindrical steatite bead.

13. Bronze fibula of twisted wire, Fig. 87 B and Pl. XIX C. This specimen is complete, although it is slightly bent so that it is no longer symmetrical. This type of fibula, of which several specimens were recovered at Vrokastro, is found over a large area; it occurred at Kavousi, *A. J. A.*, 1901, p. 136, Fig. 2; at Aigina, *op. cit.*, Pl. 116, No. 1; at the Argive Heræum, *op. cit.*, II, Pl. LXXXV, No. 830; at Thera, *op. cit.*, II, p. 300, *abb.* 489a; at Koban, *op. cit.*, Pl. 1, 3; and in Italy, Montelius, *op. cit.*, *série* A, Pl. V, 40, and *série* B, Pl. 213, No. 2.

14. Similar fibula with part of pin broken.

15. Large bronze fibula of the same type as that of Pl. XIX B but larger, Fig. 87 I.

16. Bronze fibula, Fig. 87 H. This specimen resembles that of Pl. XX, C and D, but the bow is symmetrical, the arch higher, and the central swelling larger.

---

[1] Evans, *op. cit.*, p. 71, Fig. 81a.

CHAMBER-TOMB V.

After the excavation of the tombs described, no more of this type were discovered until the last days of the campaign, when trials were made of the lower foothills west of Vrokastro. Here, on the slope Kopranes, three more were brought to light. The first of these was roughly circular in plan, its greatest width 1.66 m., length 2.09 m.; the width of the dromos was 64 m., its height 1.38 m. This tomb had evidently been rifled; not only were there vases parts of which could not be recovered, but the bones were scattered about. There is also a village tradition that the tomb had been plundered within the memory of men living. In the dromos were the fragmentary remains of a pithos; it had been lying on its side and had doubtless contained a burial. The bones from this tomb showed clear traces of burning; one skull was blackened, and many of the bones were rendered brittle by fire. The pottery from this tomb was unusually free from geometric influences. It is as follows.

1. Large bügelkanne, Fig. 89 I, of good buff clay covered with a slip which has now, however, largely chipped away. The specimen has no air-hole and has a large flat base quite unlike the slender, tapering feet of geometric bügelkannen. Horizontal bands decorate the body of the vase. On the shoulder is an irregular hatched area fringed below with a row of curls which gives the ornament some resemblance to an octopus.

2. Flask of good clay only slightly coarser than that of the above, with slip, Fig. 89 G. One handle and several pieces are missing. The ornamentation is confined to four concentric circles and a small knob on either face.

3. Smaller flask of similar clay and with similar slip,

Fig. 89 F.   This specimen has but one handle and only one face is preserved.

4. Dipper with handle in shape of bird's head, Fig. 89 D and Fig. 90.   The clay is buff and has no slip.   It is incised with horizontal and zigzag lines and the whole except the base and handle has been dipped in a black wash.   The specimen is

Fig. 89.   Pottery from Chamber-Tomb V (1 : 5).

intended to hang, not to stand.   The handle is decorated with slanting lines and the head in which it terminates is an effective bit of modeling.

5. Two-handled kylix on tall bulging foot, Fig. 89 A.   One handle is missing.   The black paint which is used for covering the interior of the vase as well as for the design is badly worn.

The shape is hardly more than a caricature of the graceful kylikes of the best Late Minoan III style.

6. Similar kylix with exactly similar design, Fig. 89 C. The paint, however, is redder.

7. Small oinochoe of poor clay, Fig. 89 B.   The design consists of horizontal bands and of a row of triangles on the shoulder.

8. Bügelkanne, with high neck and spout, sharply outlined shoulder and small foot, Fig. 89 E.   The usual air-hole occurs. The decoration consists of horizontal bands and various combinations of slanting lines.

9. Bügelkanne, corresponding to the preceding, except that the decoration in this case includes hatched triangles, Fig. 89 H.

10. Pieces of three cups like that of Fig. 79.

In addition to pottery this tomb yielded:

Fig. 90. Clay Dipper (1 : 2).

1. Iron knife, Pl. XXI A, broken into four pieces.   The tang continues the outer edge of the blade.   The cutting edge shows long use.   Cf. *Prehistoric Tombs*, p. 22, Fig. 13d.

2. Bronze earring, .023 m. diam., with curved tips which clasp, Fig. 91.

3. Similar earring with ends broken.

4. Bronze ring, inner diam. .018 m.

5. Faience beads of small disk-like type.

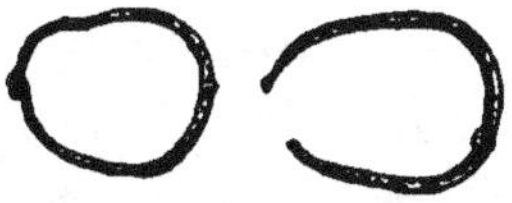

Fig. 91. Bronze Earrings (1 : 2).

6. Obsidian chips. This was the only tomb in which obsidian occurred.

7. Bronze fibula of twisted wire type like that of Pl. XIX C.

CHAMBER-TOMB VI.

The second chamber-tomb found on Kopranes had been partly demolished in recent times by the construction of a terrace wall. Remains of three skeletons were found; they showed no distinct traces of burning. The pottery resembles closely that found by Mr. Hogarth in the Knossos graves. It is as follows.

1. Large flaring bowl, Fig. 92. The inside is covered with black paint; the outside is unpainted. The handles have

Fig. 92. Vases from Chamber-Tomb VI (1 : 5).

upright pieces connecting the horizontal loops with the rim. A similar bowl was found recently in the upper stratum at Tylissos. Cf. also, *B. S. A.* VI, p. 83, Fig. 25.

2. Bird-shaped vase with three knobs for feet and a handle above, Fig. 92, 1. The vase is of poor clay and the design badly worn. It consists of bands and waved lines following the contours of the vase. The margin of the design is in one place treated in the old Minoan fashion which consists of drawing a straight and an undulating line and filling the intermediate space with black. Cf., e. g., *Sphoungaras*, p. 67, Fig. 39.

3. Similar vase less well preserved, Fig. 92, 2.   Little remains of the design, which contained, however, a good deal of cross-hatching.

4. Bügelkanne of geometric type with air-hole and knob on false spout.   Design, hatched triangles.

5. A bird-shaped vase resembling an askos, Fig. 92, 5, and constituting a type intermediate between that of Fig. 92, 1 and that of a bügelkanne.   The decoration consists of horizontal bands and hatched triangles on its upper surface.   Cf. *A. J. A.*, 1901, Pl. 1, lower row, extreme right.

Beside pottery this tomb contained the following objects.

1. Bronze ring, .013 m. diam.

2. Coiled iron ring, .013 m. diam.

3. Iron knife-end with four bronze rivets in the tang, Pl. XXI F.

4. Large bronze fibula with high forearm, Pl. XIX H. The bow is quadrangular in section and unadorned.   The forearm is sufficiently high to enclose folds of thick drapery.

Chamber-Tomb VII.

The last of the chamber-tombs to be described and the third found on Kopranes was well built and well preserved, but contained remarkably little.   Only a few bits of bones, apparently unburned, were found.   The height of the tomb as far as its roof was preserved was 413 m.; its greatest length, 2.24 m. and width, 1.59 m.   The dromos was .67 m. high and .745 m. wide. The tomb contained five vases as follows.

1. Cup of the usual geometric type.   Cf. Fig. 79.

2. Three bügelkannen, decorated with hatched triangles and provided with air-holes and knobs on their false spouts, Fig. 93.

3. Small jug, .126 m. high, decorated with hatched triangles and a waved line, Fig. 93, 1.

Two other objects from this tomb were the following.

1. Bronze ring with three coils still adhering to the finger-bone.

2. Iron spear-end, .215 m. long.

Fig. 93.   Vases from Chamber-Tomb VII (about 1 : 4).

B.   BONE-ENCLOSURES.

The type of burial to be considered next is less familiar.[1] It was of more frequent occurrence in the Vrokastro cemeteries than any other one type.   The first tombs of this type that came to light were discovered on the lower slopes of Karakovilia while the workmen were ranging about in search of other chamber-tombs.   They looked at first to be the remains of very small houses, but their very shallow depth, their small size, and the constant appearance of bones soon precluded this idea, and

[1] Apparently the burials mentioned by Mrs. Hawes in *A. J. A.*, 1901, p. 154 were of this type.

convinced us that we had to do with bone-enclosures comparable in type to those of the Middle Minoan I period discovered by the British excavators at Palaiokastro.[1]   A typical bone-enclosure is shown in Fig. 94.   It will be seen to consist of a series of small and irregularly shaped rooms, separated from one another by low walls.   The bones found within the small rooms usually bore unmistakable traces of cremation, and the pottery buried with them was, generally speaking, of a later type than that found in the chamber-tombs.

Fig. 94.   Sketch and Ground Plan of Bone-Enclosure No. 3 (Ground Plan 1 : 250).

BONE-ENCLOSURE I ON KARAKOVILIA.

The first bone-enclosure to be described was found on Karakovilia due south of Chamber-Tomb I.   It consisted of three adjoining compartments all of which contained bones, which were clearly charred.   Many bits of charred wood were also noted; in fact there was so deep and extended a deposit of black earth as to suggest the possibility of cremation having taken place on the spot.   Of the three rooms, the central was the largest; it measured 2.10 by 1.8 m. and was, on an average, .45 m. deep.   The other chambers measured, that on the east, 1.42 by 1.70 m. and was .45 m. deep; that on the west, 1.55

[1] *B. S. A.* VIII, p. 291, Fig. 5.

by .74 m. and was .24 m. deep.   In all three rooms were found potsherds in abundance.   The painted fabrics came largely from bowls and jars like those in Figs. 60 and 68.   The easternmost room contained nothing but potsherds; the central room yielded the following objects.

1. Iron sword, Pl. XXI E, badly damaged by oxidation.

2. Three iron spear-ends, Pl. XXI C, D, and H.   These, with the preceding, were found piled criss-cross.

3. Many bits of thin bronze plate and wire.

4. Crystal button.   Pieces of other buttons were noted. They had no perforations and were beveled on the surface only. They may have been used for inlay and have once adorned the box to which the foregoing bits of bronze also belonged.

5. Pieces from an iron fibula overlaid with gold-leaf. This specimen was of the same type as that in Pl. XIX D.

In the adjoining Room B were found these objects.

1. Beaded bronze fibula of the type of Pl. XX B, the coil, pin, and part of clasp lacking.   This type of fibula, conspicuous by its absence from the chamber-tombs, was frequently found in the bone-enclosures.   It may be, morphologically, a development from that of Pl. XX C, D, and F, or, as Mr. Hogarth[1] suggests, the beaded ornaments may have replaced real ornaments strung on the bow.   The type is well known and occurred at Ephesus,[2] at the Argive Heræum,[3] at Olympia,[4] and at Aigina.[5]

2. Pair of bronze tweezers or snuffers, .06 m. long.

3. Bronze pin, intact but bent, Fig. 58 D.

[1] *Ephesus*, p. 148.
[2] *Op. cit.*, Pl. XVII, 3.
[3] *Op. cit.*, II, Pl. 86, Nos. 877 and 878.
[4] *Olympia, Tafelband*, IV, Pl. 22, No. 368.
[5] *Op. cit.*, Pl. 116, 20 and 21.   Cf. also Bohlau, *Aus ionischen und italischen Nekropolen*, Pl. XV, 10.

BONE-ENCLOSURE II.

Only a few meters southwest of the bone-enclosure just described, a second was located which was found to consist, not like the foregoing of a row of rooms, but of a single chamber. Its isolation and its shape, which was very irregular, seemed due to the fact that live rock crops out on every side of this room, so that only in this one spot was the soil sufficiently deep for a grave. The bits of bones recovered from this chamber were few in number, but showed clear traces of burning. They lay loose in the earth without being enclosed in jars. No pottery was found save a few sherds which were either unpainted or showed variations of the meander motive typical of the developed geometric style.

The objects other than pottery found were as follows.

1. Iron sword, 51 m. long. Three pieces were recovered which completes the specimen save for a bit from the handle and the tip. The shape of the blade, the order of the rivets and the form of the tang correspond closely to those of the sword from Bone-Enclosure I.

2. Large bronze fibula of the geometric type with hollow bow, Pl. XX H. Parts of the clasp and pin are missing and the parts preserved contain several breaks. This fibula is noteworthy both for its size and form. Like the asymmetrical fibulæ of Pl. XIX B and H, it was designed to hold thick folds of heavy material, but unlike these it is symmetrical, for the clasp is as high as the forearm. The bow has the shape of a spoon. It is this type of fibula which has large clasps decorated with geometric ornament.[1] Undecorated examples like this

---

[1] See, e.g., *Annali*, 1880, *Tav. d'agg.* G; *Jahrbuch*, 1888, p. 362d and 363c; Ἐφ. Ἀρχ., 1892, Pl. XI, 1 and 2; *Arch. Zeit.*, 1884, Pl. 9, 3, and compare the list given in *Athen. Mitt.* XII, p. 14.

specimen have been found at Rhodes,[1] at Thera,[2] at Aigina,[3] at the Argive Heræum,[4] and at Olympia.[5]

3. Smaller bronze fibula of similar type, Pl. XX E. This specimen is of very light bronze and is badly broken. Most of the clasp is missing. The spoon-shaped bar lies in the same plane as the clasp, a variation on the preceding type which was perhaps brought about out of consideration for the wearer's comfort.

4. Still smaller iron fibula of the same type as 2, Pl. XX I.

5. Beaded bronze fibula, Pl. XX F, complete save for a part of the clasp. This type corresponds to the beaded fibula from Bone-Enclosure I, except that the central protuberance is larger than the others. A similar fibula was found at Praisos,[6] associated with pottery of a fully developed geometric style. It occurs also among the fibulæ from Aigina and from Olympia.

6. Pieces of three other fibulæ of similar type.

7. Bronze fibula, Pl. XX J, coil, pin, and part of clasp missing. This pin presents another variation of the beaded type. It resembles the pin of Pl. XX B, except that the beads are here separated by smaller disk-like protuberances.

8. Lentoid agate sealstone, sealing surface damaged, Fig. 95. The design consists of a group of fern-like devices springing from a horizontal marking and separated from one another by oval depressions. In the exergue is a double zigzag. The design shows no originality and dates from the same decadent period of gem-cutting as that shown in Fig. 88.

Fig. 95
(2 : 3).

[1] *Zeit. für Eth.*, p. 215, Fig. 17; cf. also Schumacher, *Sammlung Antiker Bronzen*, Pl. 1, No. 1.
[2] *Op. cit.*, II, p. 300, Abb. 498p.
[3] *Op. cit.*, Pl. 116, No. 3.
[4] *Op. cit.*, II, Pl. LXXXVI, No. 857.
[5] *Olympia, Tafelband* IV, Pl. XXI, Nos. 347 and 350, and Pl. XXII, No. 363.
[6] *B. S. A.* XII, p. 33, Fig. 10.

9. Two bronze fibulæ.   They are symmetrical and similar in form to the beaded fibulæ, but their bows are plain.

10. Two pendants of rock crystal.

11. Two glass beads, globular.

12. Faience bead of small disk-like shape.

BONE-ENCLOSURE III.

This is the bone-enclosure a diagrammatical sketch of which is shown in Fig. 94. It will be seen to consist of four adjacent compart-ments; in only two of these was found anything beside potsherds. In Room A, that furthest to the west, was found the amphora described below. In its mouth was a cover still adhering so tightly to the jar that it could be removed only by soaking in water. Above the am-phora was a cup of coarse clay; inside it were charred bones. We have here, therefore, a clear case of the burial of cremated remains in jars.

Fig. 96. Amphora and Cover (1 : 6).

In Room C were found other charred bones, but these were apparently buried in the earth without being enclosed in jars. The bones from the other two rooms were too few to indicate in what manner they had been interred. Potsherds from all four rooms were of the same period as the amphora.

The amphora and cover of soft pink clay are shown in Fig. 96. The painted decoration is nearly worn away on one side. It consists, as usual, of horizontal bands about the lower part of the vase and of panels of geometric ornament on the shoulder.

The neck is also painted with lines, one of which is waved.   The cover has a hatched design in the center and a row of quirks around the margin.

Besides the amphora were found an unpainted cup of coarse clay, found above the amphora, pieces of glass beads like those mentioned before, bits of iron pin like that of Fig. 58 C.

In Room C were found pieces of a heavy bronze fibula like that of Pl. XX J.

Fig. 97.   Small Jugs from Bone-Enclosure IV (about 4 : 9).

Bone-Enclosure IV.

This enclosure consisted of three rooms and corresponded in size and arrangement to Bone-Enclosure I.   All three rooms yielded potsherds in abundance; fifty per cent of these were from small jugs of light clay like those of Fig. 97, the rest of larger jars painted and unpainted.   The small vases may have been buried inside the necks of the larger ones.[1]   All bones were burned.   Two of the three rooms contained nothing beside potsherds; the third yielded the vases enumerated below.

[1] Cf. *Thera* II, p. 58.

1. Small unpainted jug of soft buff clay, ht. .065 m.

2. Small jug with flat base, Fig. 97 C. The clay is soft as in the preceding and the painted surface badly worn. The lower part of the vase is ornamented with horizontal bands, the shoulder with a row of finely hatched triangles.[1]

3. Small jug, Fig. 97 B, foot missing. The shape shows several variations on the foregoing; the neck is longer, the handle is attached not to the rim but to the neck, the body is pear-shaped, and, if M. Gilliéron's restoration is correct, the vase rests upon a foot. The decoration consists of horizontal bands between which, on the shoulder, is a row of concentric circles, and in the central zone, vertical rows of arrow ornaments.[2]

4. Small jug, Fig. 97 a, similar to the preceding in type. The shoulder is adorned with a series of volute ornaments which herald a change from the mathematical style of the geometric period. This ornament may be compared with that on a Cretan jug of the orientalizing style in the Berlin Museum, *Athen. Mitt.*, 1897, Pl. 6.

Counterparts of these vases exist in the Candia Museum; they have been enumerated and described by Professor Zahn.[3] Outside of Crete, this class of delicate little vases has been found in geometric tombs on Thera.[4] Professor Dragendorff regarded some of these as Cretan importations, others as imitations of Cretan prototypes. He suggests[5] that these jugs may mark the beginning of orientalizing influence, a suggestion supported by the decoration of the vase in Fig. 97 A. They are

---

[1] Cf. *Thera* II, p. 311, *Abb.* 4991, and two jugs in the Berlin Museum fur Völkerskunde, *Jahrbuch*, 1900, p. 53, Figs. 111 and 112.

[2] These do not appear in the illustration.

[3] See *Thera* II, p. 179, footnote.

[4] *Op. cit.*, II, p. 311; *Abb.* 499, a and c; p. 58, *Abb.* 200.

[5] *Loc. cit.*, p. 312; footnote, 27.

certainly one of the latest fabrics found at Vrokastro. Professor Dragendorff places them at the end of the eighth or the beginning of the seventh century B. C.[1]

In addition to these vases, this bone-enclosure yielded two bronze pins, to one of which a bit of wire was attached. This is one of several instances in which these pins were found in

Fig. 98. Jar from Bone-Enclosure V (1 : 2).

pairs. The piece of wire must be a remnant of the necklace or string of ornaments which passed from shoulder to shoulder and was attached to the heads of these pins. Such a necklace is clearly shown on the Francois vase.[2]

---

[1] *Loc. cit.*, p. 321.
[2] Cf. also Thiersch, *loc. cit.*, where a list of vases depicting the use of such pins is given.

BONE-ENCLOSURE V.

This, like Bone-Enclosure II, consisted of but a single room. Its contents had apparently been disturbed; only a few bits of bones were found. The objects with them were the following.

1. Part of iron blade.

2. Pieces of coarse unpainted jug.

3. Jar with horizontal handles, Fig. 98. The clay is yellow and the design-paint reddish. The decoration within the panel on the shoulder consists of two hatched butterfly ornaments so arranged against pairs of vertical lines as to give the effect of a Minoan double-axe pattern.

BONE-ENCLOSURE VI.

This bone-enclosure was only a few meters from Chamber-Tomb II. It differed from those hitherto described in that the rooms were not arranged in a single row but were irregularly placed. The rooms were shallow and were themselves of irregular outline. In Room 2 of this group was a pithos on its side containing the unburned bones of a child, which shows that in this period when cremation and interment in bone-enclosures were the rule, it was still the custom to bury children, uncremated, in jars. No indication of another burial in this room was found. In front of the pithos was noted a large flat stone which had apparently served as a lid to the pithos, but which had fallen from its original vertical position. In all the other compartments were found many bones, which, though they were not blackened as was the case in other enclosures, were, in view of their disordered arrangement and fragmentary condition, to be attributed to cremated burials. The contents of this group of rooms were as follows.

Room I.   1. Piece of a beaded fibula, Fig. 100 B.

2. Iron button with bronze center.

Room II.   In the southwest corner of this compartment, inside the pithos already described, seven articles were found.

1. Jug of soft clay, Fig. 99 C.   The lower part was once entirely covered with black paint.   A row of cross-hatched triangles with three horizontal bands complete the decoration.

2. Hydria, of somewhat better clay, with two low hori-

Fig. 99.   Vases from Bone-Enclosure VI (1 : 5).

zontal handles, Fig. 99 B.   The geometric ornament on the shoulder corresponds almost exactly to that on a jar from the town, shown in Pl. XXVII, 3.

3. Small oinochoe of similar clay, decorated with a waved line on the neck and a row of checkered triangles on the shoulder, Fig. 99 a.

4. Flaring bowl, Fig. 99 D.   As usual, the lower part of the vase is ornamented with horizontal stripes; the upper part shows concentric segments, geometrically exact.

5. Bronze fibula of symmetrical type, Fig. 100 C, like that of Pl. XX C.

6. Bronze fibula of similar type, except that the bow is more angular, Fig. 100 A.

7. Crystal bead, hexagonal in section.

Room III.   Iron spear-end, broken in three pieces, length .122 m.

Room IV.   Iron fibula of a type similar to that of Pl. XX I, but the bow is solid, not hollow.

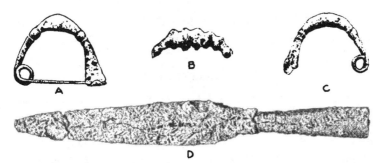

Fig. 100.   Iron Spear-end and Fibulæ from Bone-Enclosure VI (1 : 2).

BONE-ENCLOSURE VII.

This enclosure was found on Kopranes, not far from Chamber-Tomb V. It consisted of five compartments unsystematically grouped. The compartments were of irregular shapes and were placed at various levels on account of the uneven surface of the soil. The average depth of the compartments was .60 m. In one compartment was found on its side a pithos containing the unburned remains of a child. No objects were found with it. In a second compartment were bones which showed no certain traces of burning, but which, on the other hand, displayed no orderly arrangement indicating a primary burial. With them were found the following objects.

1. Flask of Cypriote type like that of Fig. 57 E. The surface is badly worn but shows traces of concentric circles of varying width and of central protuberances.

2. Bronze fibula, Pl. XIX G. This pin differs from those already described. It is not a symmetrical pin as at first appears; on the contrary, the end of the bow proper is marked by a small protuberance, the outside covering of which is several times slit open. The rest of the pin, which is thinner and flatter, belongs to the clasp.

3. Piece of bronze saw, see p. 143.

4. Iron knife, .07 m. long.

BONE-ENCLOSURE VIII.

This enclosure contained two compartments, the walls of one of which were partly broken away. The other compartment measured 2.44 by 1.31 m. and varied from .30 to .77 m. in depth. The bones were unmistakably charred. The contents of the compartment which was intact were as follows.

1. Bronze fibula of type similar to that of Pl. XX B, pin and clasp broken.

2. Large fibula of plain symmetrical flat type with plain flat bow, complete except for pin, Pl. XIX E.

3. Cylindrical bead of thin pale gold with repoussé linear design.

4. Globular bead of rock crystal.

5. Cylindrical steatite bead.

In the other compartment, the walls of which had been partly destroyed, were found the following objects.

1. Bronze fibula similar to that of Pl. XIX D, except that the flat bow is in this case in a different plane from that of the catch, Pl. XIX F.

2. Pieces of small iron saw.

BONE-ENCLOSURE IX.

This consisted of but a single room, and that partly destroyed. The signs of cremation were clear, one skull being badly charred. The only objects found in this enclosure were parts of two iron knives.

BONE-ENCLOSURE X.

This enclosure, which, again, consisted of a single room, contained bones burned to charcoal. With them occurred:

1. Part of fibula of twisted wire, type like that of Pl. XIX C.

2. Fragments of a jar of coarse clay, decorated from base to rim with horizontal stripes.

3. Unpainted bowl.

BONE-ENCLOSURE XI.

This enclosure contained bones burned to charcoal. Beside these bones there occurred the following objects.

1. Part of bronze beaded fibula like that of Pl. XX G.

2. Two bronze pins like those of Fig. 58 C. One of these has an eye just above the point; the other is broken in the middle of a similar eye. The presence of such eyes suggests that a band of ornaments was suspended not only from the heads of a pair of pins as on the Francois vase, but also that a second string of beads and pendants was held at a lower level by the eyes of such pins, although it is also possible that the string passed through these eyes was intended merely to hold the pins in position.[1]

---

[1] For other pins with eyes, see Murray, *op. cit.*, pp. 19 and 20, and Pl. VIII; *Cyprus Museum Catalog*, Pl. III, pp. 591 and 594; and *Aigina*, pp. 413 and 415.

BONE-ENCLOSURE XII.

This enclosure consists of a group of rooms irregularly orientated and shaped. They contained bones blackened by burning and also the following objects.

Room I. 1. Large open-mouthed jar, Fig. 101. Horizontal bands adorn the body of the vase; on the shoulder are painted three zigzag lines with checker pattern between them. The shape is similar to that of the vase in Fig. 61.

Fig. 101.   Krater from Bone-Enclosure XII (1 : 6).

2. Pieces of seven cups ornamented with horizontal bands and comparable to that from Courtes, shown in *A. J. A.*, 1901, Pl. IX, No. 17.

3. Amphora, Fig. 102 B, the decoration consists of horizontal bands and a row of concentric circles, two of which in each group are separated by checkers.

4. Amphora of similar shape with double handles, Fig. 102 A. The panel of decoration on the shoulder is filled, strangely enough, with a scale pattern which is entirely Myce-

næan in character. The shape of the vase, on the contrary, is geometric. A better example could hardly be found of the intermingling of Mycenæan and geometric characteristics.

Room II. Bow of bronze fibula with incised lines. It is like one in the National Museum, Athens, from Dodona.

Fig. 102. Two Amphorae from Bone-Enclosure XII (1 : 8).

Room III. Large beaded fibula, Pl. XX A.

Room IV. Jug of coarse clay with two horizontal handles and a vertical pour-handle. The lower part of the vase is decorated with closely ordered horizontal stripes; the upper part shows triangular motives. On the handle is a herring-bone pattern, Fig. 103.

In connection with these bone-enclosures it will be convenient to describe a building, the plan and photograph of which are shown in Fig. 104 and Pl. XXIV 2. It is conspicuous both by reason of its regular plan and its isolation. The fact that it was found in the neighborhood of bone-enclosures suggests that it might have been used in connection with the ritual of burial or cremation. The absence of charred remains precludes the idea that it was the place where cremation actually took place. On the other hand, the discovery close at hand of broken terra cotta figurines implies that the building contained a shrine.

Fig. 103.   Hydria (1 : 3).

It will be seen from the photograph of Pl. XXIV, 2, that the upper surface of the wall is unusually even; evidently the upper courses had been built of brick as in early Greek buildings. Further evidence for brick construction was forthcoming in four blocks of limestone which showed one or more carefully dressed surfaces. These had apparently served as jambs for the doors at either end of the building. A rebate in the surface of the block shown in Pl. XXIII, 2, seems to show that the door-posts had been made of wood.

The only two objects found in this room were a table of offerings and a krater.

1. Clay table of offerings, Fig. 105. The pieces of this table were found scattered throughout the building. Not all were recovered, several pieces of the cross supports being lacking. The object had been carefully repaired in antiquity to judge by the rivet holes which were noted in several places

on the legs. On the top of the table was painted a large rosette.[1]

The other object from this building is the krater of Fig. 106. Several pieces and most of the foot are lacking. This vase is an example of the fully developed Dipylon style. Almost its entire surface is covered with black paint; the only exceptions are three groups of narrow bands about the body, and

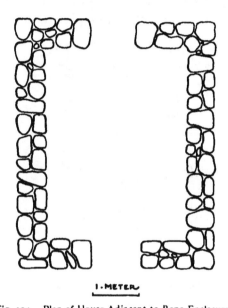

I·METER

Fig. 104.   Plan of House Adjacent to Bone-Enclosures.

the background of the closely ornamented panel on the shoulder. The double handles and the ribbed foot are both characteristic of this class of geometric vases. The clay of which this vase

[1] It is possible that the geometric sherds mentioned on p. 243 of B. S. A. VIII "from plates with low vertical sides, decorated on the exterior with large rosettes" may be from similar tables rather than from plates. I know of no clay tables analogous to this specimen; clay tripods or vase supports with openwork bases are fairly frequent, see B. S. A. VIII p. 250, Fig. 21, and Annals of Archaeology, III, Pl. XXIX, No. 20, and Ἐφ. Ἀρχ., 1898, Pl. 4, No. 3.

is made is the hard reddish clay very similar to that of the bowl in Pl. XXVI.[1]

The fragments of figurines found in the vicinity of this building were a part of a human figure, a part of a duck and a part of a figurine of a horse.

PITHOS-BURIALS.

Burials in jars have already been noted in connection with the Vrokastro houses, the chamber-tombs, and the bone-

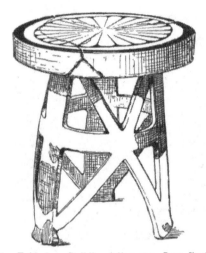

Fig. 105. Clay Table from Building Adjacent to Bone-Enclosures (1 : 5).

enclosures. Three other instances of such burials in jars remain to be enumerated, which were unassociated with either tombs or houses. Two were located on one of the eastern spurs of Vrokastro, to which the natives have given the name, Khavga (Χαυγά); in a circular pit cut from the hard white soil. One pithos was on its side, and contained the unburned bones and the teeth of a child. The mouth of the jar was closed with two

[1] For a ribbed base with rectangular perforations see, e. g., a krater from Melos published in *Jahrbuch*, 1899, Vol. XIV, p. 34, Fig. 11, and *ibid.*, p. 80, Fig. 33.

large disks of stone like those found in the Vrokastro houses
and in Chamber-Tomb I.   The other jar appeared at a lower
level and, like Minoan burial jars, was inverted and wedged
into position by large stones.   The bones inside were those
of an adult; they showed no traces of burning.   The only
object found with this burial was the bügelkanne of Pl. XXVII, 1.

Fig. 106. Geometric Krater from Building Adjacent to Bone-Enclosures
(about 1 : 4).

It has the usual air-hole on the shoulder and knob on the false
spout.   Its decoration presents close analogies to that of the
pottery from Chamber-Tomb I; the fern-like fringe on the
hatched triangles and the solidly black triangle are both characteristic of the earlier phase of Cretan geometric style, of
which the best examples were afforded by the pottery from
Chamber-Tomb I.

The other jar-burial was found adjacent to Chamber-Tomb IV on Amigdali. The pithos was on its side and contained the unburned remains of an adult. One cup and two bits of perforated steatite made up the burial gifts.

INTERMENT ROCK-SHELTER.

Lastly, in enumerating the various types of interments found on Vrokastro, mention should be made of a burial under an overhanging ledge of rock which runs along the southern edge of the Karakovilia slope. Several skeletons had been interred here; that they belonged to the geometric period was certain, for geometric sherds and a small unpainted jug like that of Fig. 99 C were found with them.[1]

---

[1] Cf. Mr. Hogarth's brief description of geometric cave-burials in Zakro, *B. S. A.* VII, p. 148 and *B. S. A.* XII, p. 3.

CONCLUSION.

The proportion of incineration and of inhumation in the tombs described may be readily seen in the accompanying diagram.   In cases where the number of skeletons could be

	CHAMBER-TOMBS.							BONE-ENCLOSURES.											
	1	2	3	4	5	6	7	1	2	3	4	5	6	7	8	9	10	11	12
Inhumated Skeletons........	Child's	24	7				3						Child's	Child's					
Skeletons in Jars......	.			1	1														
Doubtful................ ..	+		+			+													
Cremated Remains in Earth.	+			+	+			+	+	+	+	+	+		+	+	+	+	+
Cremated Remains in Jars...	3			+					+										

Diagram Showing the Relation of Incineration and Inhumation in the Burials at Vrokastro.

observed the number is noted in the diagram, otherwise the occurrence of a given type of burial is indicated by a cross. When the bones are those of a young child, that fact is also noted.   The liabilities to error in these observations are chiefly two: it is possible that cremated remains found loose in the earth had once been enclosed in jars, inasmuch as fragments of pottery were invariably found with the ashes and all pottery was broken.   This, however, seems improbable in view of the fact that the bones were themselves so scattered.   Again it is possible that distinction was not correctly drawn between burned and unburned bones.   The difference between bones from which the flesh has been burned away and those from which the flesh has decayed away is a slight one, and it is unnecessary to suppose that the fire in every case devoured the bones. This difficulty has, however, been at least partially obviated by relegating to a doubtful class the cases where the signs of burning were not unmistakable. Counting out such doubtful cases and also child-burials, the proportion of cremation in the chamber-tombs was fifty per cent; in the pithos-burials, which were distinct from tombs, cremation does not occur; in the bone-enclosures it reaches one hundred per cent. The natural inference from these facts is, of course, that the bone-enclosures are later than the built tombs. Until cremation had been universally adopted, chamber-tombs were still built for the dead, but when entire skeletons were no longer buried, and less space was needed, the simpler and easier method was adopted of burying ashes in the small compartments of bone-enclosures.

If now this supposition be correct and the bone-enclosures are later than the tombs, the difference in method of burial will furnish what the stratification of Vrokastro did not, a line of demarcation between the earlier and later phases of the geometric civilization. It remains to review the pottery and bronzes to see if differences are observable.

One difference is salient. The bügelkanne which occurred in every chamber-tomb except No. 4, which, it will be remembered, was nearly empty, did not once occur in the bone-enclosures. Other shapes reminiscent of Mycenæan ceramic art and frequent in the chamber-tombs were lacking in the enclosures. These were the kylix, the askos, and the duck-shaped vase. With the exception of one flask from Bone-Enclosure VII and of one krater from Bone-Enclosure XII, these shapes were also lacking in the later type of interment. Types of pottery characteristic of the enclosures were the hydria, the geometric amphora, and the small jugs of Fig. 97. The potsherds from these burials indicated that bowls with panel decoration were also characteristic. A comparative study of shapes, however, indicates neither that there was a hard and fast line between the ceramic art of the two periods, nor that separate interments of the two types were of the same date. Several shapes, the cup of Fig. 79, the small oinochoe, the flaring bowl, Fig. 99 D, are common to both. So indeed is the geometric type of amphora, although it is noteworthy that both this shape and the hydria occurred but once in the chamber-tombs and that in No. III which contained much less that was reminiscent of Mycenæan art than the others.

As regards design, it is observable that the ornament is applied to vases from the tombs less compactly than to those from the enclosures. Together with this close style of ornament goes a tendency to confine the ornament to a panel and to cover the rest of the vase either with solid black or with closely drawn horizontal bands.

It must be admitted, however, that the force of these conclusions is somewhat weakened by the fact that the pottery from the enclosures was much less numerous than in the chamber-tombs. Fibulæ, on the other hand, were even more numerous, and the evidence afforded by them accords with that yielded by the pottery. Two types frequent in the enclosures were absent in the built tombs. These are the symmetrical beaded fibula, Pl. XX A, B, G, and J, and the geometric fibula of Pl. XX E, H, and I. Morphologically, these types are both developments from a plainer type of pin like that of Pl. XX C, D, and F, found in the tombs.

We are thus warranted, I believe, in dividing the geometric remains of Vrokastro into an earlier and a later period according to the method of burial practiced. Whether such a division will hold good for other Cretan sites of the iron age is uncertain. Both at Courtes and Rusty Ridge, Kavousi, vases of the fully developed geometric style were found in chamber-tombs. There is, however, a possibility that tombs built in the period of the quasi-geometric style were re-used in the succeeding era. Moreover, there is some evidence that elsewhere also a difference in method of burial differentiated these two periods. Mr. Hogarth found vases parallel to those from the bone-enclosures in "an oblong pit, roofless," which he seems to distinguish from tholoi. This may indicate another modification of the earlier chamber-tomb now rendered superfluous by the universal adoption of cremation.

But even if there shall be found to be local variations as to the time when chamber-tombs were abandoned and as to the type of tomb which succeeded them, this will not impair, I believe, the usefulness of the distinction indicated by the evidence at Vrokastro.

Questions of chronology now confront us. Before considering them it may be well to review the successive periods which have been traced at Vrokastro. The Middle Minoan period, since it is separated from the subsequent history of the site which chiefly concerns us by the long interval of the Middle Minoan III, the Late Minoan I, and the Late Minoan II periods, may be dismissed with two observations: First, that the fact of a Middle Minoan settlement on Vrokastro is at variance with the current view that Minoan sites are to be found in low-lying areas; and second, that it is rare to find in eastern Crete pottery of the Middle Minoan period without finding above it pottery of the Late Minoan period.

Perhaps it was only the people of this latter period who did not live on hills.

We come now to the main settlement on Vrokastro which lasted from the end of the bronze age nearly to the dawn of classical Greece.   Three periods may be distinguished; they are as follows.

I. The late Mycenæan period represented by the pottery from below floor levels in the town.   Associated with this pottery were the fibulæ of Pl. XIX A and B.   This period was not represented in the tombs at Vrokastro, but at other Cretan sites have been found larnakes and chamber-tombs of this era.[1]   This pottery is analogous to the L. M. IIIb class of Mr. Dawkins, to the reoccupation style of Gournia, and to that of Tomb B at Mouliana.[2]   Some of this pottery is classed by Dr. Mackenzie as Achæan and is grouped by him with the succeeding division of our classification.   That the closest relation exists between these two classes is indisputable and that Achæan influence had already made itself felt, is probable, but the fact (a) that this pottery differs materially from that found in the chamber-tombs at Vrokastro, and (b) that pottery of this type is not usually found associated with cremated burials, warrants, I believe, its separation· from pottery of the period of the quasi-geometric style.

II. The period of the quasi-geometric style, represented by the pottery from the chamber-tombs, which was associated with both cremated and uncremated remains, and with iron implements.   The fibulæ of this period are those intermediate

---

[1] Boyd-Hawes, *Gournia*, pp. 45 and 46; *B. S. A. VIII*, p. 303.

[2] The cremated remains in Tomb A at Mouliana belong, apparently, with the pottery shown in Ἐφ. Ἀρχ., 1904, p. 27, Fig. 6.

between the fiddle-bow type and the beaded fibula. Emphasis may again be placed on the prevalence during this period of the Cypriote type of krater, which, as Dr. Mackenzie suggests, brings this class into connection with the warrior vase of Mycenæ. In Crete, pottery of this type has been found in Tholos 6 at Knossos,[1] in the earlier tombs of Kourtes,[2] at Erganos,[3] at Thunder Hill, Kavousi,[4] and at Patela.[5] Outside Crete the closest parallels are to be found at *Salamis*,[6] at Assarlik,[7] and at Skyros and Theotoku in Thessaly.[8]

III. The geometric period represented by the pottery from the bone-enclosures. This pottery in shape and decoration is analogous to that found in the Dipylon cemetery, on Thera, and other geometric sites. It is invariably associated with cremated remains. The fibulæ of this period include the types of the foregoing period and also the beaded and geometric types.

In determining the date of this last period, the close correspondence of the fibulæ from the enclosures with those found in Schiff's grave on Thera is of prime importance. All types found in the Theran grave are present in the enclosures with the exception of the spectacle type and the *kleinasiatisch* fibula.[9] The absence of these implies that the Vrokastro enclosures are slightly earlier in date than the Theran tomb, which was assigned by Dragendorff to the seventh century.

[1] *B. S. A.* VI, p. 84.
[2] *A. J. A.*, 1901, Pl. VIII.
[3] *ibid.*
[4] *Id.*, Pls. I and II.
[5] *A. J. A.*, 1897, p. 252.
[6] Wide, *loc. cit.*
[7] *J. H. S.* VIII, p. 69, Figs. 4-8.
[8] Wace and Thompson, *op. cit.*, pp. 208-216, and p. 255.
[9] *Loc. cit.*, p. 300; *Abb.*, 489, t-w.

The resemblance of the small jugs of Fig. 97 to those from Schiff's grave confirms this conclusion.   At Aigina, beaded fibulæ were assigned to the end of the eighth and the beginning of the seventh century.[1]   The spectacle fibula is generally held to date from the early part of the seventh century B. C.[2]   We, therefore, obtain as provisional dates for the third period the eighth century B. C.   If the absence of the spectacle fibula be a matter of chance, an even later date might be assigned.

The best evidence for dating the period of the quasi-geometric style is afforded by the tripod from Chamber-Tomb I and by the fibulæ.   Accepting Furtwängler's date for the Enkomi tripod as about 1000 B. C., we may assign the second class of pottery to the beginning of the first millennium B. C., and, allowing an equally long interval for either division of the geometric style, we obtain 1000–850 B. C. as provisional dates for the period of the quasi-geometric style and 850 to 700 B. C. for the period of the mature geometric style.

Of still more absorbing interest than chronological problems are questions of ethnology.   If geometric pottery be held in general to be the product of the Dorian race, then the third period represents the Dorian invasion of Crete.   The pottery of the first period, in view of its resemblance to mainland types, must be assigned to the Mycenæans.   Yet even in this period a new influence is observable.   Mr. Dawkins and Dr. Mackenzie have shown that the introduction of a Cypriote type of krater and of the geometric type of bowl indicate affinities[3] with the succeeding period.   This new influence I believe Dr. Mackenzie right in ascribing to the Achæans.   To the

---

[1] *Aigina*, pp. 474–475.
[2] *B. S. A.* XIII, p. 72.
[3] *B. S. A.* IX, p. 320 and *id.*, XIII, p. 434.

Achæans then may be provisionally assigned the quasi-geometric pottery of the second class.[1]

If these theories be correct, the remains of Vrokastro record three great invasions of Crete from the North, those of the Mycenæans, the Achæans, and the Dorians.

---

[1] Further evidence for this theory is afforded by the excavations carried on by Messrs. Wace and Thompson at Halos in Achaia Phthiotis, where pottery has come to light, which bears the closest resemblance to that from Vrokastro. I regret that the very useful article in *B. S. A.* XVIII, pp. 1-29 reached me so late as to make it impossible to compare the two wares in detail.

APPENDIX.

NOTE ON AN EARLY MINOAN II CAVE-BURIAL AT AYIOS ANDONI.

In 1912, while the weather was still so unsettled as to prevent pitching camp on Vrokastro, trial excavations were conducted in the neighborhood of Kavousi.   Along the bed of the river which runs to the north of the village were found several rectangular chamber-tombs analogous to those described in the foregoing report but containing little else than fragments of bones and small bügelkannen of poor clay.   Of greater interest was an Early Minoan II burial located in a cave-like recess on the steep hillside immediately above the little church of Ayios Andoni (Ἅγιος Ἀντόνι).

The objects found in this grave were as follows.

1. Veined marble bowl, intact, ht. .67 m., diam. .127 m.

2. Fragments of an alabaster jug similar to that published by Mr. Seager in *Explorations on the Island of Mochlos*, Pl. V, VI, 2.

3. Sherds of Early Minoan II red and black mottled ware; of a fine polished gray ware; and of Early Minoan III light on dark ware.

4. Clay pot with suspension handles of reddish ware, ht. .063 m.

5. Small jug of red clay, ht. .105 m., similar to that published by Mr. Seager, *loc. cit.*, Fig. 7, II b.

6. Three-legged cooking-pot, ht. .094 m.

7. Large gourd-shaped vase, ht. .137 m., with suspension

handles.   The objects other than pottery from this tomb are shown in Fig. 107.   They are as follows.

1. Steatite beads of various shapes, conspicuous among which are three cylindrical beads with ribbed surface.

2. Two bronze blades, closely analogous to blades from Mochlos, *loc. cit.*, Fig. 45.

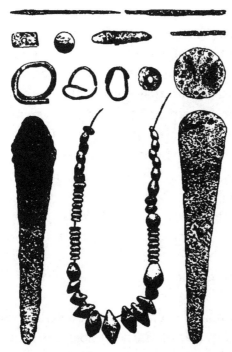

Fig. 107.   Early Minoan II Objects from a Cave Burial at Ayios Andoni near Kavousi (2 : 3).

3. Silver disk with central and marginal perforations.

4. Bronze borers.

5. Ivory pendant in the form of a pig, Fig. 108.

6. Three curls, two of silver, one of bronze, for confining locks of hair.   These curls are similar to those found in the

second stratum at Troy (W. Doerpfeld, *Troia und Ilion, Beilage* 43, p. 352 and p. 358), and furnish accordingly further evidence for equating the second stratum at Troy with the Early Minoan period in Crete.

Fig. 108.   Ivory Pig from Cave Burial, Ayios Andoni, near Kavousi (2 : 3).

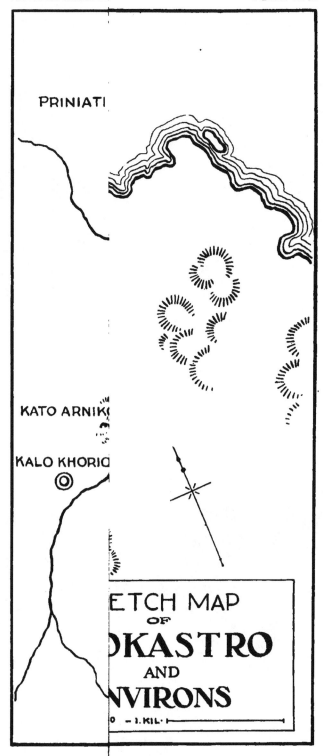

PRINIATI

KATO ARNIK(

KALO KHORIO

ETCH MAP
OF
OKASTRO
AND
NVIRONS

0 — 1. KIL·

PLATE XVIII.

ANTHROPOLOGICAL PUB. UNIV. OF PA. MUSEUM, VOL. III.

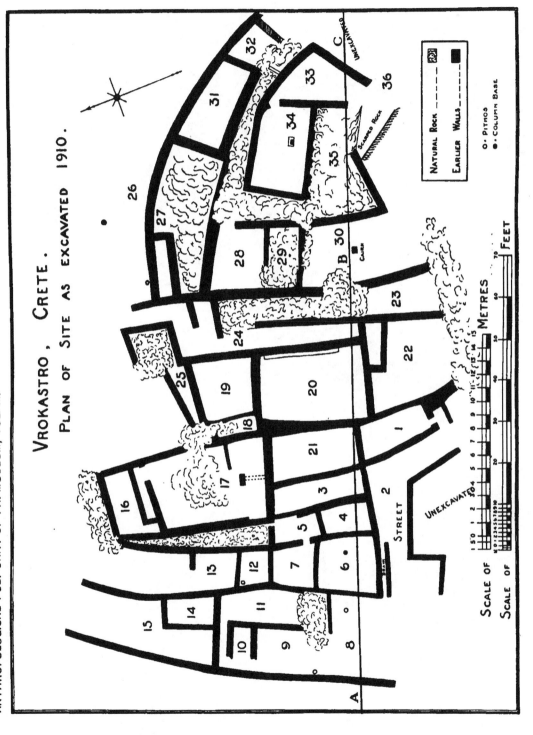

VROKASTRO, CRETE.

PLAN OF SITE AS EXCAVATED 1910.

NATURAL ROCK

EARLIER WALLS

O: PITHOS

●: COLUMN BASE

SCALE OF METRES

SCALE OF FEET

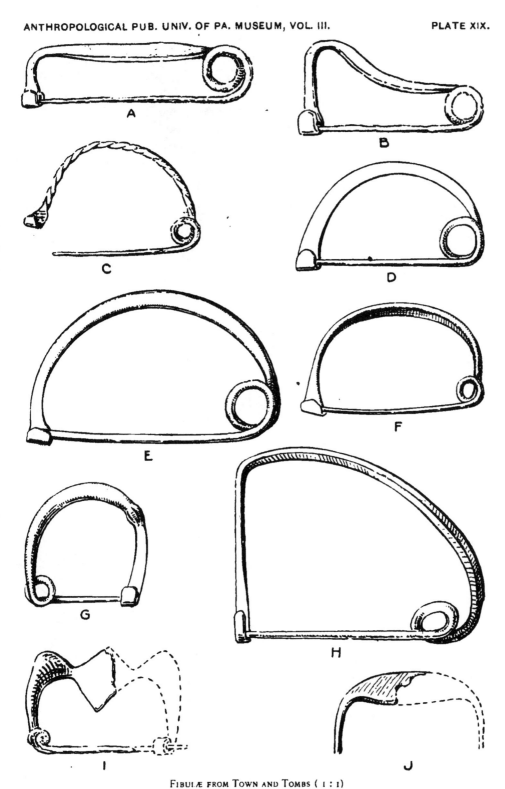

FIBULÆ FROM TOWN AND TOMBS (1 : 1)

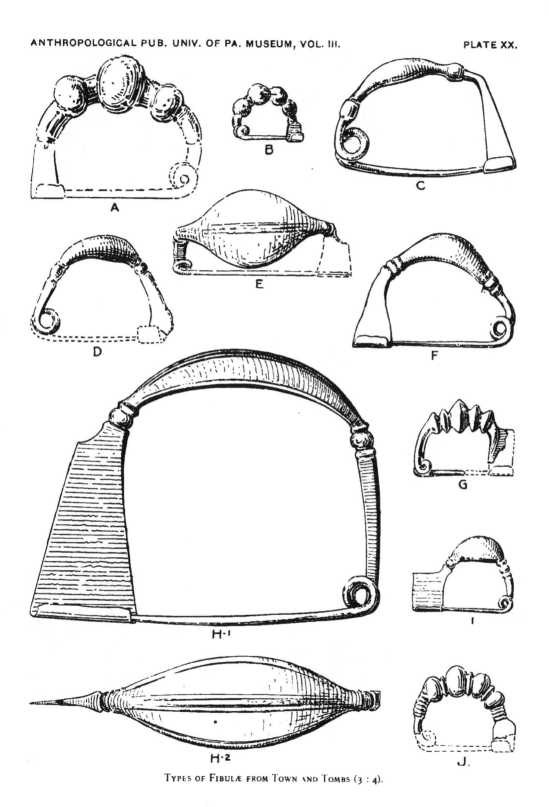

TYPES OF FIBULÆ FROM TOWN AND TOMBS (3 : 4).

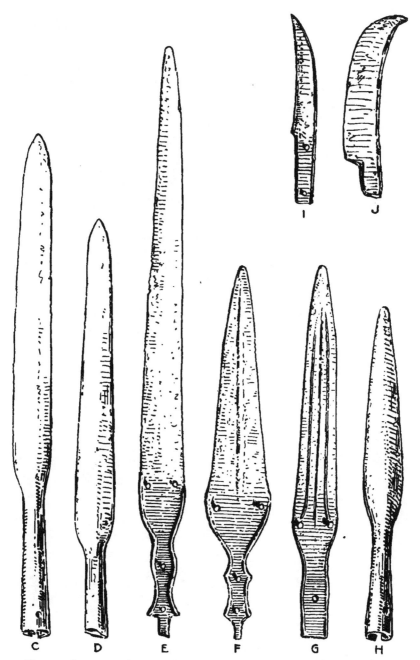

TYPES OF BRONZE AND IRON BLADES FROM TOWN AND TOMBS (1 : 2).

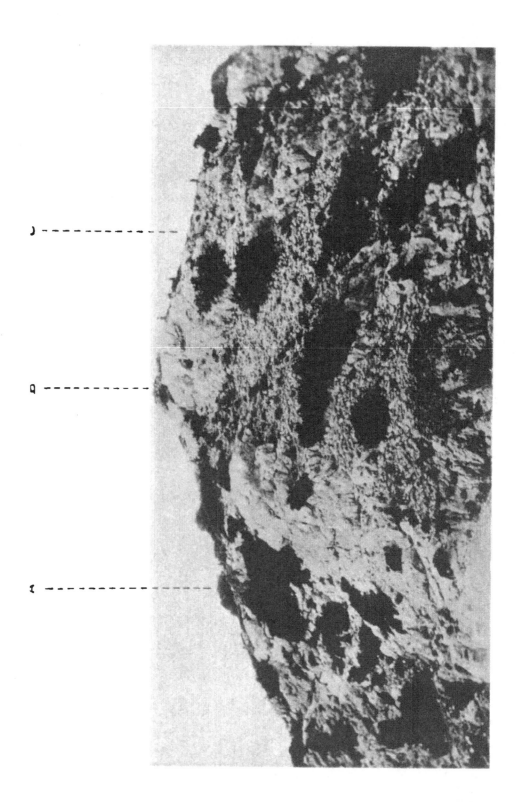

1. VIEW OF EXCAVATED ROOM, VROKASTRO, SHOWING THE ROUGH LEDGES ABOVE WHICH FLOORS WERE BUILT.
2. BLOCK OF DRESSED LIMESTONE FROM BUILDING NEAR BONE-ENCLOSURES, KARAKOVILIA.

DOORWAY OF HOUSE, VROKASTRO

BUILDING ADJACENT TO BONE-ENCLOSURES.   KARAKOVILIA.

1. MIDDLE MINOAN JUG FROM LOW LEVEL OF ROOM 27, VROKASTRO. SCALE 1 : 2.
2. KYLIX PAINTED IN THE QUASI-GEOMETRIC STYLE FROM CHAMBER-TOMB I. KARAKOVILIA. SCALE 1 : 2.

BOWL OF THE MATURE GEOMETRIC STYLE FROM ROOM 22, VROKASTRO. SCALE 1 : 2.

1. BÜGELKANNE FROM PITHOS-BURIAL, KHAVGA. SCALE 1 : 2.
2. BOWL AND COVER FROM CHAMBER-TOMB III, KARAKOVILIA. SCALE 1 : 2.
3. HYDRIA FROM TOWN, VROKASTRO. SCALE 2 : 5.
4. OINOCHOE FROM CHAMBER-TOMB III, KARAKOVILIA   SCALE 2 : 5.

AMPHORA OF THE MATURE GEOMETRIC STYLE. VROKASTRO.   SCALE. I : 5.

1. BOWL OF THE QUASI-GEOMETRIC STYLE FROM CHAMBER-TOMB I, KARAKOVILIA SCALE
2. BOWL OF THE QUASI-GEOMETRIC STYLE, VROKASTRO. SCALE 1 : 2.

AR OF THE QUASI-GEOMETRIC STYLE FROM CHAMBER TOMB I, KARAKOVILIA.   SCALE 1 : 4.

AMPHORA OF THE QUASI-GEOMETRIC STYLE FROM CHAMBER TOMB I,
KARAKOVILIA. SCALE I : 2.

BRONZE TRIPOD FROM CHUNGUL KURGAN. HEIGHT 91.7 cm.

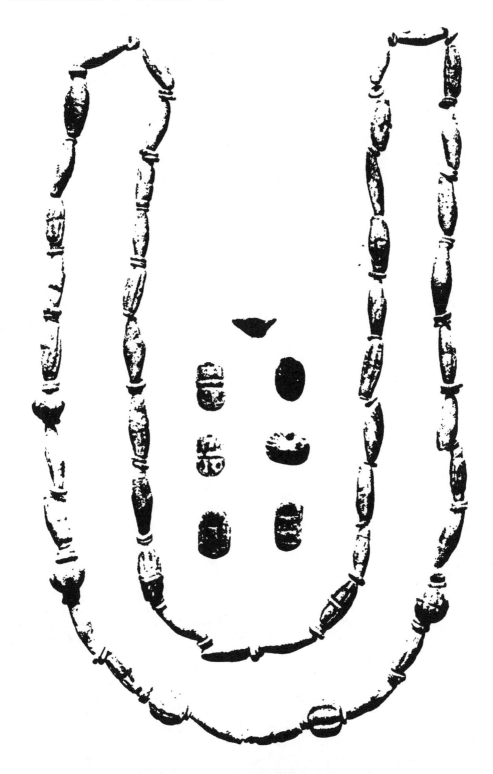

FAIENCE BEADS AND SEALS FROM CHAMBER TOMB I. KARAKOVILIA
AND CHAMBER TOMB IV AMIGTHALI   SCALE I : 2.

CPSIA information can be obtained
at www.ICGtesting.com
Printed in the USA
LVHW101638020321
680382LV00006B/371